State Census Records

S·T·A·T·E
CENSUS
RECORDS

Ann S. Lainhart

Published by Genealogical Publishing Co., Inc.
1001 N. Calvert St., Baltimore, Maryland 21202
Second printing 1993
Third printing 1994
Fourth printing 1997
Library of Congress Catalogue Card Number 92-72944
International Standard Book Number 0-8063-1362-5
Made in the United States of America

PREFACE

In 1986 I began transcribing and publishing the 1855 and 1865 Massachusetts state censuses. As a result of my work I was asked to speak on state censuses at the convention held by the Federation of Genealogical Societies in Boston in 1988. Since I had personal knowledge of the state censuses of only Massachusetts, Rhode Island, and New York, I began preparing for my lecture by looking at what was in print on state census records in general. I quickly found that much of this material was misleading at best and wrong at worst.

Aware of the problems with the information in print on state census records, I wrote to the archives, state library, or state historical society of each state that was supposed to have censuses and received a vast amount of useful information in reply. For the convention I compiled all this information into a small book. Although it served its purpose at the time, I soon realized that in order to have a fully comprehensive book on the subject of state censuses I would need help and advice from more than just state institutions. For this present edition, therefore, I resolved to seek the advice of specialists. Genealogists and local historians have an intimate knowledge of their own fields, often surpassing the expertise even of state and local officials, so with the invaluable assistance of many such specialists throughout the country — as well as the continued assistance of state institutions — I have now updated, revised, and expanded the 1988 booklet, transforming it out of all recognition.

Up until now the principal sources for information on state censuses have included the following five works: (1) Alice Eichholz, *Ancestry's Red Book, American State, County & Town Sources* (Salt Lake City, 1992); (2) Arlene Eakle and Johni Cerny, *The Source* (Salt Lake City, 1984); (3) a list that appears in the front of the federal census indexes published by Accelerated Indexing Systems of Bountiful, Utah (hereafter AIS); (4) John F. Valentine, "States and Territories, Census Records in the United States," *Genealogical Journal*, 2 (1973); and (5) Henry J. Dubester, *State Censuses, An Annotated Bibliography of Censuses of Population Taken After the Year 1790 by States and Territories of the United States* (Washington, D.C., 1948). A few examples will show how information in these books is sometimes misleading or wrong.

Massachusetts began taking state censuses in 1855 and took them every ten years through 1945, but the original population schedules survive only for the years 1855 and 1865. For the other years there are published statistical summaries based on the census, but no original returns.

Three of the above sources list these post-1865 Massachusetts censuses but fail to tell the reader that the original returns do not exist.

The Source lists state censuses for New Hampshire every ten years from 1855 through 1895, but these do not exist and never did.

The "Schedule of Colonial, Territorial, and State Census Records" which appears in many of the AIS indexes, lists the years that such "census records" were supposedly taken. For fifteen states (Connecticut, Delaware, Kentucky, Maine, Massachusetts, New Hampshire, New Jersey, New York, North Carolina, Pennsylvania, Rhode Island, South Carolina, Tennessee, Vermont, and Virginia), plus the District of Columbia, the year 1798 is listed. I have yet to find a census taken in 1798, though there was a Federal Direct Tax levied that year. This was a tax on dwelling houses and listed the owner or tenant of every house. While it does list the names of many people in each of these states, it was not in fact a census. Other years listed in the AIS schedule may be for sources other than census records.

Many published books use the word census in the title even though the material in the book does not originate from any kind of census. *The 1776 New Hampshire Census* (Jay Mack Holbrook [Holbrook Research Institute], 1976) is a listing of those men who signed the Association Tests. *The Census Tables for the French Colony of Louisiana From 1699 Through 1732*, by Charles R. Maduell, Jr. (Baltimore, 1972) does contain some censuses in its list of sources, such as "Census of the Inhabitants of the First Settlement on the Gulf Coast, Fort Maurepas, December, 1699," but it also contains sources such as "List of Marriageable Girls Who Arrived Aboard the Pelican" and "List of Officers Commissioned at Fort Louis." The fact that these books contain information from sources that are not technically censuses certainly does not lessen their value, but it does point up the difficulty in knowing just what to include in a book on state censuses.

This book is about *state* census records and therefore includes only censuses taken after the formation of the United States. However, territorial censuses have also been included, as many of these were taken to prove there was sufficient population to warrant statehood. For colonial census records the reader is directed to Evarts B. Greene and Virginia D. Harrington's *American Population Before the Federal Census of 1790* (New York, 1932).

The following are the states for which no state or territorial census appears to be extant: Connecticut, Idaho, Kentucky, Montana, New Hampshire, Ohio, Pennsylvania, and Vermont. One exception is Maryland which enumerated its population in 1776, technically before statehood, but since it was so close to statehood, it has been included in this book. In a few cases I have included information on other sources such as the Quadrennial Enumerations in Ohio and the Great Registers (voters' lists) in Arizona. But in general I have avoided references to those records that can be used as census substitutes, such as tax lists and voters' lists. Where original census records are notably deficient, however, I have drawn attention to *published* substitutes and "reconstructed" censuses as a convenience to the reader.

Although in each state section I have acknowledged individual researchers and genealogists who gave so generously with their help, I want to say again how grateful I am for their assistance. Their personal knowledge has added immeasurably to the accuracy and comprehensiveness of this book, making it, I hope, a valuable resource for all researchers interested in state census records. I especially want to thank Gordon Remington who has looked over the whole book and made many helpful suggestions and additions.

Ann S. Lainhart

INTRODUCTION

Researchers may quite rightly ask why we should concern ourselves with state censuses when federal censuses are so widely and readily available. There are several answers to this question. State censuses may fill in gaps left by missing federal censuses. State censuses may not be closed to the public for a seventy-two year period as are federal censuses; in fact some state censuses taken as recently as 1945 are available to the public. Many state censuses ask different questions than federal censuses, so you may find information about your ancestors that would never be found in the federal records. And finally state censuses can help fill out the picture of your ancestors and help solve genealogical problems.

The biggest gap in federal census records was occasioned by the loss of most of the 1890 census. Many state or territorial censuses were taken in 1885, 1892, and 1895 and can fill in the twenty-year gap in the federal censuses (1880-1900). Examples of some of the states with censuses for these years are Colorado (1885), Florida (1885, 1895), Iowa (1885, 1895), Kansas (1885, 1895), Nebraska (1885), New Jersey (1885, 1895), New Mexico (1885), New York (1892), North Dakota (1885), Rhode Island (1885), South Dakota (1885, 1895), and Wisconsin (1885, 1895). The 1850 census is missing for a few California communities, but there is an 1852 California state census; and the 1870 census for Arapahoe County, Kansas, is missing, but there are state censuses for both 1865 and 1875. These few examples demonstrate how state censuses can be used to fill in the gaps in federal censuses.

This year, in observance of the seventy-two year restriction period, the 1920 federal census was opened to the public, but some of the more recent state censuses are already available to researchers. The following states have such censuses: Florida (1935, 1945), Iowa (1925), Kansas (1925), New York (1925), North Dakota (1925), Rhode Island (1925, 1935), and South Dakota (1925, 1935, 1945).

Many state censuses ask different questions than those asked in the federal censuses. In 1865 the Massachusetts state census asked males if they were legal voters or naturalized voters; knowing that your ancestor had been naturalized by 1865 can help you narrow the search in locating that naturalization record. The 1935 and 1945 Florida censuses ask for the "degree of education." The 1925 Iowa census asks for names of parents (including mother's maiden name) and place of marriage of parents. The 1875 through 1925 Kansas censuses ask "where from to Kansas (state or country)." The 1855, 1865, and 1875 New York censuses list county of birth for those born in New York, and the 1865 Rhode Island census lists the town of birth for those born in Rhode Island. Many post-Civil War state censuses ask for information about veterans, some even asking for the regiment and company in which they had served.

Using state censuses to fill out the picture of a family may help solve a genealogical problem. An example is the family of Peter and Ann. I was asked by a client to find the death record of Peter; she had found Peter in the 1865 Rhode Island state census as age 45. She had found the death records of two Peters of the right surname in Rhode Island, but for neither of them did their age at death figure back to a birth year of 1820. So she wanted me to find the correct death record. Knowing that the ages given in census records can often be inaccurate, I began with a complete census search on Peter and Ann. I found them in the following censuses with the following ages:

> 1850 Federal census for Blackstone, Massachusetts
> Peter, 30
> Ann, 30
> 1855 State census for Blackstone, Massachusetts
> Peter, 30
> Ann, 27
> 1860 Federal census for Blackstone, Massachusetts
> Peter, 30
> Ann, 34
> 1865 State census for Scituate, Rhode Island
> Peter, 45
> Ann, 39
> 1870 Federal census
> family not yet found
> 1880 Federal census for Smithfield, Rhode Island
> Peter, 50
> Ann, 55

The names of the children were consistent in all these entries and the surname unusual enough that it was clear it was the same family. This was the only family of this surname in Smithfield in the 1880 census, and one of the death records that the client had already found was for a Peter who died in Smithfield in 1881 age 52. All along the client had the information she hired me to find!

As with any census records, those produced by the states may also contain instances where the enumerator added information that was not called for but which can be extremely valuable to later researchers. I have found several such cases in the census records of the seventy-one towns I have transcribed in Massachusetts. There are twenty-two towns in 1855 and ninety-six towns in 1865 where the enumerators entered specific town of birth instead of just state or country. In some cases this can include the town, parish, or county of birth in another country.

Sometimes the enumerator added some special comments. One noted in the 1865 census of Hanson, Massachusetts, that 91-year-old Hannah Barker was the "Oldest person in town, retaining *all* her mental faculties; Eyesight good." In 1865 Winchester the birthplaces of two of the children of Isaac N. Knapp, sea captain, are listed as "At Sea Ship Kentucky," and "At Sea Ship Wm. Chamberlain." And in 1865 South Reading (now Wakefield) the birthplace of 4-year-old Harry W. Smalley was explained this way:

> In Gulf of Siam in a Peruvian Ship under a Spanish Captain, three
> hours after the loss of the vessel in which the Mother sailed from the
> U.S.

In the 1865 New York census for Granville, Washington County, the enumerator wrote in the margin next to the Winchell family: "These 11 live in a little Shanty 12 by 12 only one Room, how they sleep is a puzzle to me I think they can't all get in at once."

Genealogists working with nineteenth-century material know how helpful middle names can be in identifying ancestral families. But so often sources, including censuses, just give middle initials. Then, of course, there are enumerators like Samuel Hosmer who took the 1855 census in Acton, Massachusetts. He wrote out the full name of everyone! These include Napoleon Bonaparte Puffer, Sarah Eunice Appleton Brabrock, Harriet Anngernett Wheeler, Thomas Green Fesenden Jones, Maria Hildreth Tuttle, Theodore Cleaveland Fletcher, and Charles Augustus Bailey Carter Brown. Spot-checking showed that in many cases the middle names given for married women were their maiden names.

Users of this book should note that at the beginning of most of the state sections, the repository is listed where the manuscript copies (I refer to them as the original copies) of the state censuses are located. Much of this material has been microfilmed, but it can be necessary at times to check the original source. Researchers may find microfilm copies of state censuses at other repositories in the state, but it would be too cumbersome to indicate where all available copies are to be found. Much of this material is also available on microfilm through the Family History Library (FHL) in Salt Lake City, and those not available at the FHL have been so noted in the text.

Researchers should also be aware that Accelerated Indexing Systems has begun to include in their recent indexes to the 1890 veterans census a "Selected Bibliography of Similar Subject Matter and Background Sources." This includes published books and articles on censuses, both state and federal, of that particular state.

State census records can help to fill in the full picture of our ancestors and in many cases provide information not available anywhere else. These censuses may not be as readily available nor as fully indexed as the federal ones, but they are certainly worth the extra effort it may take to use them. It is hoped that this book will aid the researcher in knowing where to look and what to look for in state censuses.

ALABAMA

The 1820 territorial census of Alabama is extant for Baldwin, Conecuh, Dallas, Franklin, Limestone, St. Clair, Shelby, and Wilcox counties, and is published in Marie Bankhead Owen, *Alabama Census Returns 1820 and An Abstract of Federal Census of Alabama 1830* (Baltimore, 1967).

State censuses are available for the following counties for 1855 and 1866. The censuses name the head of household only.

1855:

Autauga	Lowndes	Sumter
Baldwin	Macon	Tallapoosa
Blount	Mobile	Tuscaloosa
Coffee	Montgomery	Wilcox
Franklin	Perry	
Henry	Pickens	

This census has been published by Ronald Vern Jackson, *Alabama 1855 Census Index* (AIS, 1981).

1866:

Autauga	Henry	Pickens
Baldwin	Jackson	Pike
Bibb	Jefferson	Randolph
Blount	Lauderdale	Russell
Butler	Lawrence	Shelby
Calhoun	Limestone	St. Clair
Clarke	Lowndes	Sumter
Coffee	Macon	Talladega
Conecuh	Marengo	Tallapoosa
Coosa	Marion	Tuscaloosa
Covington	Marshall	Walker
Dale	Mobile	Washington
Dallas	Monroe	Wilcox
Fayette	Montgomery	Winston
Franklin	Morgan	
Greene	Perry	

The territorial and state censuses are located at:

Reference Division
Alabama Department of Archives and History
624 Washington Avenue
Montgomery, Alabama 36130

There is also a 1907 census of Confederate veterans.

13

Dr. Thomas M. Owen's *History of Alabama and Dictionary of Alabama Biography* says: "The official State census was originally instituted solely for the purpose of securing a basis for apportionment of representation in the legislature. Enumerations were made with regularity until 1855. The first census classified the population with respect to families, sex, persons over twenty-one years of age and those under twenty-one, free persons of color, and the total number of slaves. With the development of the State the need for more detailed data became manifest, and the scope of the enumerations was somewhat expanded, later censuses including, in addition to the foregoing, data as to the number of colleges, academies and common schools in each county, and the number of pupils in each; the number of white children of school age; and the number of insane persons, epileptics and idiots, mutes, blind persons, crippled and maimed persons in every county. It does not appear, however, that possessions or property, occupations, or other data of an economic character were ever shown in the State census reports."

ALASKA

From David Hales, "Genealogy Sources in Alaska," *The Sourdough,* [University of Alaska, Fairbanks] 20(1983):17:

In October, 1879, Major John C. Tidball, commander of the Sitka Post, ordered a census of the civilian population, excluding natives. This census was recently included in: DeArmond, Robert N., ed. LADY FRANKLIN VISITS SITKA, ALASKA, 1870: THE JOURNAL OF SOPHIA CRACROFT, SIR JOHN FRANKLIN'S NIECE. Anchorage, Alaska: Alaska Historical Society, 1981. The census includes 391 individuals, with name, age, birthplace, occupation, and remarks: "house clean, comfortable, handsomely fixed," "worthless, lazy ex-soldier," "freshly married," and "orphan." Occupations noted were "sailmaker," "laundress," "carpenter," "prostitute," "seamstress," "thief and rascal."

Buried in early U.S. Commissioner of Fisheries reports are census records for native inhabitants of Saint Paul and Saint George Islands. The records include names of individuals, grouped by families, age at last birthday, and place of birth. These reports are:

ALASKA FISHERIES AND FUR INDUSTRIES IN 1914: APPENDIX IX TO THE REPORT OF THE U.S. COMMISSIONER OF FISHERIES FOR 1914. (Bureau of Fisheries Document No. 819) Washington, D.C.: Government Printing Office, 1915. (Contains census records of the native inhabitants of St. Paul and St. George Islands as of June 30, 1914.)

ALASKA FISHERIES AND FUR INDUSTRIES IN 1917: APPENDIX II TO THE REPORT OF THE U.S. COMMISSIONER OF FISHERIES FOR 1917. (Bureau of Fisheries Document No. 847) Washington, D.C.: Government Printing Office, 1918. (Contains census records of the native inhabitants of St. Paul and St. George Islands as of May 31, 1917.)

Census records for 1878 are also available for Unalaska, other Aleutian Island villages, and mainland Aleut villages of Belkofski, Micholayevsk, and Protassof (Morzhovoi). The records of each village are grouped under "Church officials and families," "Creoles," "widows and orphans," and "Aluets." Only the full name of the head of household is listed with other family members referred to as "his child," or "his wife," etc. The age of all family members is given and a running tally is kept showing the sex of individuals listed and total number of males and females in each village.

Ronald Vern Jackson has published *Alaskan Census Records 1870-1907* (AIS, 1976), and *The Source* lists the following printed censuses:

> 1881. Sitka only; printed *House Exec. Doc. 5*, 42nd Cong., 1st sess., serial 2027.
> 1885. Cape Smyth, Point Barrow; printed *House Exec. Doc. 44*, 48th Cong., 2nd sess., serial 2298.
> 1890-95. Pribiloff Islands; printed *House Exec. Doc. 92*, pt. 1, 55th Cong. 1st sess., serial 3576.
> 1904. School Report, Saint George and Saint Paul Islands, *Senate Doc. 98*, 59th Cong., 1st sess., serial 4911.
> 1905. Saint George and Saint Paul Islands, same vol. as 1904.
> 1906-07. Saint George, Saint Paul Islands, *Senate Doc. 376*, 60th Cong., 1st sess., serial 5242.

Copies of the federal censuses for 1880, 1890, and 1900 only are to be found at:

> State of Alaska
> Department of Education
> Division of State Libraries
> Alaska State Library
> Post Office Box G
> Juneau, Alaska 99811-0571

There is a very interesting article based on the journal of Maurice Johnson who took the 1900 census covering the lower Yukon and Kuskokwin rivers: Dorothy Jean Ray, "Taking the Census in 1900," *Alaska Sportsman* (October 1968).

ARIZONA

Some of the state censuses are located at:

Archives and Public Records
Arizona State Archives
Department of Library, Archives and Public Records
1700 W. Washington
Phoenix, Arizona 85007

As of the date of this publication, the State Archives Division was in the midst of a reprocessing project and the censuses were not in a unified series. Some of the censuses are on microfilm, some in the records of the Secretary of Arizona Territory, and some in the Archives Division. Below is a listing of each county and the years for which there are either censuses or great registers (registers of voters, much like census records because the data is similar). Most of these censuses and great registers are not available at the FHL; however, they do have the 1866 census for the counties of Mohave, Pah Ute, Pima, Yavapai, and Yuma.

Apache:	Census 1880, 1882
	Great registers 1884, 1888, 1890, 1892, 1894, 1896, 1898, 1900, 1902, 1904, 1906, 1907, 1908, 1909, 1910, 1912
Cochise:	Census 1882
	Great registers 1882, 1884, 1894, 1896, 1902, 1906, 1908, 1910, 1912-1934
Coconino:	Great registers 1894, 1902, 1906, 1908, 1910, 1911
Gila:	Census 1882
	Great registers 1882, 1888, 1894, 1896, 1898, 1900, 1902, 1904, 1906, 1908, 1909, 1910
Graham:	Census 1882
	Great registers 1882, 1889, 1894, 1902, 1906, 1910, 1911
Greenlee:	Great registers 1911
Maricopa:	Census 1872, 1874, 1876, 1882
	Great registers 1872, 1874, 1876, 1878, 1880, 1882, 1890, 1894, 1895, 1900, 1902, 1904, 1906, 1908, 1909, 1910, 1911, 1912-1938
Mohave:	Census 1866, 1867, 1872, 1874, 1876, 1880, 1882
	Great registers 1882, 1894, 1902, 1906, 1908, 1911
Navajo:	Great registers 1895, 1896, 1898, 1900, 1902, 1904, 1906, 1908, 1910, 1912, 1913, 1914, 1916, 1918, 1920, 1922-24, 1926, 1928, 1930, 1932, 1942

Pah Ute:	Census 1866
Pima:	Census 1866, 1867, 1872, 1874, 1876, 1882
	Great registers 1876, 1880, 1882, 1884, 1885, 1886, 1888, 1890, 1892, 1894, 1896, 1898, 1900, 1902, 1904, 1905, 1906, 1908, 1910, 1912
Pinal:	Census 1876, 1882
	Great registers 1882, 1894, 1902, 1906, 1908, 1910, 1911
Santa Cruz:	Great registers 1902, 1906, 1908, 1910
Yavapai:	Census 1866, 1869, 1872, 1874, 1876
	Great registers 1882, 1886, 1890, 1892, 1894, 1896, 1900, 1902, 1904, 1906, 1908, 1910-1915
Yuma:	Census 1866, 1867, 1872, 1874, 1876, 1882
	Great registers 1882, 1886, 1894, 1896, 1902, 1906, 1908, 1910-1915

The state censuses and great registers for the following counties and years are at the Arizona State Archives:

Apache:	Great registers 1884-1910
Cochise:	Census 1882
	Great registers 1882-1910, 1912-1934
Coconino:	Great registers 1894-1911
Gila:	Census 1882
	Great registers 1882-1910
Maricopa:	Census 1872-1882
	Great registers 1876-1938
Mohave:	Census 1866-1882
	Great registers 1894-1911
Navajo:	Great registers 1895-1932
Pima:	Census 1866-1882
	Great registers 1876, 1880, 1882
Pinal:	Census 1876-1882
	Great registers 1894-1911
Yavapai:	Census 1866-1876
	Great registers 1882-1908, 1910-1915

Many thanks to Linda S. McCleary for her help with this section.

ARKANSAS

The sheriff's censuses for 1823 and 1829 and the 1865 state census are located at:

Arkansas History Commission
One Capitol Mall
Little Rock, Arkansas 72201

Sheriff's censuses were taken in 1823, 1825, 1827, and 1829, but only those for the years 1823 (Arkansas County only) and 1829 are available.

The 1829 Sheriff's Census is complete for the following counties (these are not available at the FHL):

Arkansas	Crawford	(Old) Miller
Chicot	Crittenden	St. Francis
Clark	Independence	Washington
Conway	Lawrence	

The inhabitants of these counties were usually enumerated by township. Only the name of head of household is listed, with the rest of the household divided into the following categories:

Free white males:	of 45 years and upwards
	of 21 years and upwards
	of 18 years and under 45
	under 21 years
Free white females:	of 16 years and upwards
	under 16 years
Free colored persons:	males
	females
Slaves:	of 45 years and upwards
	of 10 years and under 45

No records have been found for Pope and Sevier counties, and names were not submitted for the counties of Hempstead, Izard, Lafayette, Phillips, and Pulaski. The above two censuses have been indexed in Ronald Vern Jackson and Gary Ronald Teeples, *Arkansas Sheriff's Censuses 1823 & 1829* (AIS, 1976).

The 1865 state census exists only for Washington County. It gives the names of heads of households and the following information:

Free white males:	under 10
	over 10 and under 18
	over 18 and under 21
	over 21 and under 45
	over 45
Free white females:	under 16
	over 16
Free persons of color:	males
	females
Acres of land in cultivation:	in cotton
	in grain
Production:	bales of cotton
	bushels of corn
	bushels of wheat
	bushels of oats

A sheriff's census was also taken in 1854, but no copies of the actual returns are known to exist. A statistical summary of this census can be found in the *Journal of the Senate of the Tenth Session of the General Assembly of. . . Arkansas* (Little Rock, 1855), Appendix pp. 111-113.

There is also a 1911 enumeration of Confederate veterans that was to be taken by each county's tax assessor. Records survive for forty-four counties and have been published in Bobbie Jones McLane and Capitola Glazner, *Arkansas 1911 Census of Confederate Veterans*, 3 vols. (1977-81). Bobbie Jones McLane has also compiled *An Index to the Three Volumes: Arkansas 1911 Census of Confederate Veterans* (available from Arkansas Ancestors, 222 McMahan Drive, Hot Springs, Arkansas 71913). These records usually include the name of the veteran, his address, date and place of birth, date and place of enlistment, names and birthplaces of the veteran's parents and grandparents, maiden name of wife, the date and place of their marriage, names of her parents, and a list of children.

Many thanks to Carolyn Earle Billingsley for her help with this section.

CALIFORNIA

The state and Mexican mission censuses are available at:

California State Archives
1020 O Street, Room 130
Sacramento, California 95814

The *Historical Society of Southern California Quarterly* has published several early California padrons (censuses) for the year 1790. These padrons contain name, age, occupation, marital status, and the town of nativity:

Los Angeles 41(1959):181
The Royal Presidio of San Francisco 41(1959):386
Santa Barbara 42(1960):90
Monterey 42(1960):210
Presidio of San Diego 43(1961):107

Volume 18 (1936) of the *Quarterly* is a special edition containing a complete facsimile reproduction of the 1836 Padron of Los Angeles and the surrounding jurisdiction. This padron contains the name, age, community of residence, occupation, town of nativity, marital status, and a check whether man, woman, or child (children reached majority at 12). There is no index to the names. And in volume 42 (1960), there is a transcription of the 1844 Padron of Los Angeles and the surrounding jurisdiction. This padron is in the same format as 1836. There is an index following the transcription.

In addition, the *Quarterly* published in volume 43 (1961) an 1816 list for Los Angeles residents which provides their names, name of spouse, date of entry to Los Angeles, land owned, and occupation.

Four early mission censuses — San Carlos 1796, San Luis Obispo 1797-8, Soledad 1798, San Antonio 1798 — are kept at the State Archives and microfilm copies are available for public use. All of these censuses are arranged in columns containing only the name and age of those enumerated. Most of the entries are for Indians and only the given name is provided. Separate sections are made for each of the following headings: Religious, Married Couples, Widows, Widowers, Unmarried Men, Unmarried Women, Boys, Girls, and New Born Infants. The State Archives also has an eight-page manuscript census for the presidial districts of San Diego, Santa Barbara, Monterey, and San Francisco in 1788. The census provides the total number of men, women, boys, and girls at each presidio and mission and for the pueblos of Los Angeles and San Jose. These totals are listed under two headings, "Indians" and "Spaniards & Other Races." There is also a one-page census for the Villa of Branciforte dated 31 December 1798 which names nineteen settlers with the number of livestock they own and the amount of corn, wheat, and beans produced each year.

The 1852 Special Census of California was required by the California Constitution of 1849, which states in Article IV ". . . A census is required to be taken in 1852, in 1855 and every ten years thereafter. . ." It has been suggested that the 1852 census was taken as a result of the inadequacy of the 1850 census which did not record the residents of three of the then existing twenty-seven counties, namely Contra Costa, San Francisco, and Santa Clara. These three counties represented a substantial portion of the population of California in 1850 (especially San Francisco, then the largest urban population in California), and the loss of that information is a tremendous blow to early statehood research. Fortunately, the 1852 census fills the gap, but the 1852 Special Census was not the result of the missing 1850 data. It was a result of the recognition that the population of California was changing rapidly because of the gold rush and the government of California would need to adapt to this rapid change. The decision to take this census was made prior to the 1850 federal census, and in fact prior to statehood. However, the 1852 census was the only one taken as required by the state constitution; no other state censuses were ever taken.

The 1852 Special Census is similar in format to the 1850 federal census with one major and important difference: instead of an estimate of the property value, the previous residence of each individual is recorded. This allows a researcher to follow family migrations and possibly locate a family elsewhere in 1850 prior to their arrival in California. Columns were also included to indicate citizenship, race, and foreign birth.

The original and a microfilm copy of the 1852 census are at the California State Archives, with another microfilm copy at the California State Library. In addition to the original records, the DAR made a typescript copy in thirteen volumes, each covering different counties or parts of counties. Each volume contains an index to its contents (there is no consolidated index). The DAR typescript does not include the many Chinese residents of California. A problem with the typescript is the way in which each volume was paged and indexed. It is almost impossible to use the typescript to locate the same page for a better reading in the original since the order of pages in the typescript is different from the original order and there is no cross reference. Also, pages that were difficult to read in the original were not transcribed by the DAR.

Several local census records are also housed in the State Archives. They are not considered official census records and contain little information. The following such censuses have been microfilmed and are available at the FHL:

Chico, Butte Co., 1906. Alphabetized by the first letter of the surname, typewritten, and contains name only.

Greenview Township, Siskiyou Co., 1908. In household order, typewritten, and contains name, town of residence, and age.

Kern, Kern Co., 1908. Alphabetized by the first letter of the surname, handwritten, and contains name and street address.

Long Beach, Los Angeles Co., 1905. Alphabetized by the first letter of the surname, handwritten, and contains name, street address, sex, occupation, and age.

Long Beach, Los Angeles Co., 1906. Alphabetized by the first letter of the surname, handwritten, and contains name, street address, sex, occupation, and age.

Long Beach, Los Angeles Co., 1908. Alphabetized by the first letter of the surname, typewritten, and contains name and street address.

Los Angeles, Los Angeles Co., 1897. The census is in alphabetical order, typewritten, and contains only the name and street address.

Monrovia, Los Angeles Co., 1910. Alphabetical order, typewritten, and contains name and street address.

Oakland, Alameda Co., 1902. Alphabetized by the first letter of the surname, typewritten, and contains name only.

Porterville, Tulare Co., 1908. Alphabetical order, typewritten, and contains name only.

Red Bluff, Tehama Co., 1908. Alphabetical order, typewritten, and contains name, age, sex, occupation, and street address.

Richmond, Contra Costa Co., 1908. Alphabetical order, typewritten, and contains name, age, sex, and street address.

San Buenaventura, Ventura Co., 1905. Alphabetized by the first letter of the surname, typewritten, and contains name only.

San Diego, San Diego Co., 1899. Alphabetized by the first letter of the surname, typewritten, and contains name and street address.

San Jose, Santa Clara Co., 1897. Alphabetical order, typewritten, and contains only names.

San Luis Obispo, San Luis Obispo Co., 1906. Alphabetized by the first letter of the surname, typewritten, and contains name, sex, age, and street address.

San Pedro, Los Angeles Co., 1906. Alphabetical order, typewritten, and contains only names.

Santa Monica, Los Angeles Co., 1905. Alphabetical order, typewritten, and contains name and street address.

Scotts Valley Township, Santa Cruz Co., 1908. In household order, typewritten, and contains name, community of residence, and age.

The following volumes are not microfilmed but are available at the State Archives (these are not available at the FHL):

Adin - Lookout, Modoc Co., 1938. Alphabetical order, typewritten, and contains name, street address, age, occupation, and place of birth (state or country).

Albany, Alameda Co., 1926. Alphabetical order, typewritten, and contains name only.

Anaheim, Orange Co., 1916. Alphabetical order, typewritten, and contains name only.

Anaheim Township, Orange Co., 1919. Alphabetical order, typewritten, and contains name only.

Beverly Hills, Los Angeles Co., 1926. Alphabetical order, typewritten, and contains name and street address.

Burbank, Los Angeles Co., 1925. Alphabetized by the first letter of the surname, typewritten, and contains name only.

Calexio, Imperial Co., 1919. Alphabetical order, typewritten, and contains name only.

Cedarville Township, Modoc Co., 1922. Alphabetized by the first letter of the surname, typewritten, and contains name only.

Compton, Los Angeles Co., 1924. Alphabetized by the first letter of the surname, typewritten, and contains name and street address.

Fresno, Fresno Co., 1914. Alphabetical order, typewritten, and contains name, age, sex, street address, and occupation.

3rd Judicial Township, Glenn Co., 1916. Alphabetical order, typewritten, and contains name only.

Glendale, Los Angeles Co., 1912. There is only a cover letter summarizing the population by precinct.

Huntington Beach, Orange Co., 1924. Alphabetical order, typewritten, and contains name and street address.

Huntington Park, Los Angeles Co., 1921. Alphabetized by the first letter of the surname, typewritten, and contains name only.

Inglewood, Los Angeles Co., 1924. Alphabetical order, typewritten, and contains name, address, race, age, occupation, and sex.

Laguna Beach Township, Orange Co., 1934. Alphabetical order, typewritten, and contains name only.

Judicial Townships 3, Merced Co., 1916. Alphabetical order, typewritten, and contains name only.

Judicial Townships 2, Merced Co., 1918. Alphabetized by the first letter of the surname, typewritten, and contains name only.

Judicial Townships 5, Merced Co., 1918. Alphabetized by the first letter of the surname, typewritten, and contains name only.

Judicial Townships 6, Merced Co., 1919. Alphabetical order, typewritten, and contains name only.

Judicial Townships 8, Merced Co., 1919. Alphabetized by the first letter of the surname, typewritten, and contains name only.

Judicial Townships 8, Merced Co., 1923. Alphabetized by the first letter of the surname, typewritten, and contains name only.

Monterey Park, Los Angeles Co., 1925. There is only a cover letter summarizing the total population of 5,130.

Newport Beach Township, Orange Co., 1934. Alphabetical order, typewritten, and contains name only.

Pacific Grove, Monterey Co., 1926. Alphabetized by the first letter of the surname, typewritten, and contains name only.

Pittsburg, Contra Costa Co., 1918. Alphabetical order, typewritten, and contains name only.

Pittsburg, Contra Costa Co., 1922. Alphabetical order, typewritten, and contains name only.

Redondo Beach, Los Angeles Co., 1919. Alphabetical order, typewritten, and contains name, age, street address, sex, and race.

Tulare, Tulare Co., 1921. Alphabetized by the first letter of the surname, typewritten, and contains name only.

Tulelake Township, Modoc Co., 1938. Alphabetized by the first letter of the surname, typewritten, and contains name, community of residence, occupation, age, and place of birth (state or country).

Venice, Los Angeles Co., 1914. Alphabetical order, typewritten, and contains name and street address.

Watsonville, Santa Cruz Co., 1912. Alphabetical order, typewritten, and contains name, age, color, and sex.

Westwood Township, Lassen Co., 1916. Alphabetized by the first letter of the surname, typewritten, and contains name only.

Woodland, Yolo Co., 1918. Alphabetized by the first letter of the surname, typewritten, and contains name only.

In addition to the above census records the State Archives also has the following:

San Francisco, 1880. A handwritten population summary by precincts and wards.

1890 Federal Census "Misc. Materials". A population summary by the five Supervisors' Districts, the counties within each Supervisor's District, and the Assembly District, Supervisory District or Township within each county.

El Centro, Imperial Co., 1977. A cover letter summarizing the population at 22,660.

1940 Lassen, Plumas, Shasta, Sierra, Siskiyou, Tehama, Trinity, and Modoc counties. A summary of the population and the number of farms by township in each of these counties.

Many thanks to Jim W. Faulkinbury, C.G.R.S, for his help with this section.

COLORADO

The 1861 Poll Book, 1866 census, and 1885 Special Federal Census are located at:

Colorado State Archives
Room 1B-20
1313 Sherman Street
Denver, Colorado 80203

A general election was held in Colorado on 19 August 1861. In poll books, officials recorded the names of voters, so while this is not a true census, it does document Colorado residence. At the date of this publication the 1861 Poll Book for Colorado was being indexed by the Computer Interest Group of the Colorado Genealogical Society.

The State Archives has ten handwritten sheets of a population enumeration taken prior to 23 June 1866 for northeastern Colorado. This includes the present counties of Logan, Morgan, Phillips, Sedgwick, and Weld, and parts of Washington and Yuma. There is a published index: Arliss Shaffer Monk, *Index to a Weld County Census, Colorado Territory, 1866* (1978). The enumeration lists heads of household only, with the rest of the household divided into white males over and under age twenty-one and white females over and under age eighteen.

The 1885 Special Federal Census Schedule includes four schedules: population, agriculture, industrial, and mortality. The National Archives has microfilmed these returns and copies are also available at the State Archives and the National Archives/Rocky Mountain Region. The headings for the population schedule are: name of street, house number, dwelling house in order of visitation, family number, name of each person, color, sex, age, born within the census year (give month), relationship to head, marital status, profession, number of months unemployed, sick or disabled, blind, deaf, dumb, idiotic, insane, crippled, whether attended school, if can read and write, place of birth, place of birth of father and mother.

An actual index to this 1885 census is not yet available. There does exist at the State Archives and the National Archives/Rocky Mountain Region a microfilmed version of the enumerations of some counties which is loosely referred to as an "index." Many genealogists also mistake it for the original census. This "index" arranges inhabitants within a county alphabetically by the first letter of their surname and includes partial information such as name, age, birthplace, and marital status. In some counties, initials are used almost entirely in place of given names, although the original census may show names rather than initials. This "index" appears to be the abbreviated, state-level copy of the more complete census that went to Washington. Unfortunately, this partially-alphabetized version does not give a reference to the corresponding page number of the federal return. Currently, the Colorado Council of Genealogical Societies is coordinating a project to compile a statewide index to the full census.

The following is a list of the counties included in the 1885 census. An asterisk (*) denotes those counties for which the separate partial census exists, arranged by letter of the alphabet. These are available on microfilm through interlibrary loan for a fee.

Arapahoe*	Elbert	Mesa*
Archuleta	El Paso*	Montrose
Bent	Fremont*	Ouray
Boulder	Gilpin*	Park*
Chaffee*	Grand	Pitkin
Clear Creek	Gunnison*	Pueblo
Conejos*	Hinsdale	Rio Grande*
Costilla	Huerfano*	Routt
Custer*	Jefferson*	Saguache
Delta*	Lake*	San Juan
Dolores*	La Plata	San Miguel
Douglas*	Larimer	Summit
Eagle*	Las Animas*	Weld*

Many thanks to Kathleen W. Hinckley, C.G.R.S, C.G.L., for her help with this section. See her article "Genealogical Research in Colorado," *National Genealogical Society Quarterly,* 77(1989):107.

DELAWARE

In January of 1782, the General Assembly ordered tax collectors to take a census and by November the census had been completed. Complete population returns exist for only six hundreds: Brandywine, Christiana, and St. George's hundreds in New Castle County; Duck Creek and Little Creek hundreds in Kent County; and Lewes Town Hundred in Sussex County. These list the name of the head of household and group other members of the household by males over and under eighteen and females over and under eighteen. There are population totals only for these hundreds: Mill Creek, White Clay, New Castle, Red Lion, and Pencader in New Castle County; St. Jones (Dover) and Mispillion in Kent County; and Broadkill, Cedar Creek, Dagsberry, Indian River, North West Fork, and Nanticoke in Sussex County. Harold B. Hancock has published *The Reconstructed Delaware State Census of 1782* (Wilmington, 1983).

FLORIDA

Existing state censuses are located at:

Public Records Unit
Florida State Archives
Department of State
R.A. Gray Building
Tallahassee, Florida 32399-0250

Richard Roberts in his article "Florida's State Census Records," *The Florida Genealogist*, 13 (1990), says that the 1885, 1935, and 1945 "censuses are some of the most under-utilized records in Florida genealogical research." Information on both state and federal censuses is also to be found in Brian E. Michaels' article "Genealogical Research in Florida," published in the *National Genealogical Society Quarterly*, 76(1988):89.

Persons using the Florida state census records need to be flexible when researching locations. The population tended to move around, and researchers should be prepared to search surrounding counties if a family is not found where they are "supposed" to be. The following is a list of the remnants of the earlier censuses that still exist and the missing precincts from the 1935 and 1945 enumerations. The FHL does not have the 1855, 1866, 1867, 1935 and 1945 censuses:

1825:   Leon County, published in Dorothy Dodd, "The Florida Census of 1825," *Florida Historical Quarterly*, 22(1943):34.

1845:   County recapitulation only, no names.

1855:   Gadsden County
        Marion County, published in Brian E. Michaels, "Marion County in the 1855 State Census," *The Florida Armchair Researcher*, 1(1984):24.
        Franklin County, June 1855. A census of children between the ages of five and eighteen.

1866:   Franklin County. A census of children between the ages of five and eighteen, published in "Franklin County Children Ages 5-18 in 1866," *The Florida Armchair Researcher*, 1(1984):7.

1867: Franklin County, fragments.
 Hernando County, fragments.
 Madison County, fragments.
 Orange County, fragments.
 Santa Rosa County, fragments.

1868: Levy County (listed at FHL).

1875: Alachua County

1885: Originals of this census are in the National Archives in Washington, D.C. A microfilm copy is at the State Archives and the Florida State Library. This census includes population, mortality, agricultural, and industrial schedules. The schedules for Alachua, Clay, Columbia, and Nassau counties are missing. The population schedule for Putnam county has been published in *The Putnam County Genealogical Society Quarterly Journal*, volume 3 (1986). William T. and Patricia Martin have prepared an every-name index of 312,551 entries for this census (for further information write to them at 3735 South Lake Drive, Miami, FL 33155-6644). There may be problems with using the page numbers in this index since there is more than one set of microfilms for the 1885 census, but the Martins have issued an Addendum to aid researchers using a different set of films.

1895: Nassau County has been published by the Jacksonville Genealogical Society, 4589 Amherst Street, Jacksonville, Florida 32205.

1905, 1915, 1925: No original records have been found. Published tabulations are in the Florida documents section of the Florida State Library.

1935: Enumerations for each county are in the Florida State Archives. These records are arranged alphabetically by county and then geographically by election precincts. Enumerations give the following information: name, address, inside or outside of city limits, age, sex, race, relation to family, place of birth (state or country), degree of education, own or rent home, and occupation. No index is available. The user needs to know the 1935 election precinct number, which in most cases can be obtained from county supervisors of elections. The smaller counties, though, are not difficult to search without a precinct number. These enumerations are not available at FHL.
 The following precincts are missing from these counties:
 Alachua: 4, 5, 18, 21
 Baker: 6

Bradford: 1
Citrus: 13
DeSoto: 6, 7
Duval: 14A, 36
Flagler: 2, 6
Lee: 20
Levy: 12
Liberty: 5
Martin: 7
Nassau: 4
Orange: 1-10
Palm Beach: 9
Polk: 19, 23, 34
St. Johns: 19
Sarasota: 5
Walton: all missing

1945: Enumerations for each county are in the Florida State Archives. These records are arranged alphabetically by county and then geographically by election precincts. Enumerations give the following information: name, address, inside or outside of city limits, age, sex, place of birth (state or country), degree of education, and occupation. No index is available. The user needs to know the 1945 election precinct number, which in most cases can be obtained from county supervisors of elections. The smaller counties, though, are not difficult to search without a precinct number. These enumerations are not available at FHL.
The following precincts are missing from these counties:
Alachua: 18
Bay: 8, 9, 12
Citrus: 13
DeSoto: 6, 7
Gadsden: 2
Highlands: 8
Liberty: 3
Orange: 1-11
Palm Beach: 27, 29, 34
Polk: 34
Seminole: 15
Volusia: 14
Washington: 18

Many thanks to Linda Pazics Kleback for her help with this section.

GEORGIA

Original and microfilm copies of many of the state censuses are located at:

Secretary of State
Georgia Department of Archives and History
330 Capitol Avenue S.E.
Atlanta, Georgia 30334

Counties named below are the only ones with extant censuses for that
particular year:

1798: Part of the 1798 census for Greene County is in Greene County
File, File II Counties, at the Archives. It was published by Frank
Parker Hudson, "1798 Census of First Battalion, Greene County,
Georgia," *Georgia Genealogical Society Quarterly*, 4 (1968): 649.

1800: Oglethorpe County's census is in the courthouse and a copy is on
microfilm at the Archives. It was published by Mary Bondurant
Warren, *1800 Census of Oglethorpe County, Georgia* (Athens, 1965).

1810: The statistics from the state census of that year (which coincided
with the 1810 federal census) were published in *Columbian Museum and Savannah Advertiser*, Savannah, 19 November 1810.

1824: The statistics for this census were published in the *Southern Recorder*, Milledgeville, 21 December 1824.

1827: Taliaferro County's original census is in the courthouse; a copy is
on microfilm at the Archives. It is included in *Censuses for
Georgia Counties* (Atlanta, 1979). The statewide statistics for this
census were published in the *Southern Recorder*, Milledgeville,
28 November 1829.

1831: The statistics for this census were published in the *Southern Recorder*, Milledgeville, 8 December 1831.

1834: The Cass (Bartow), Cherokee, Cobb, Forsyth, Gilmer, Lumpkin,
Murray, and Union County censuses are in the Telamon Cuyler
Collection, Hargrett Rare Books and Manuscripts Library, Uni-

versity of Georgia Libraries. They are included in Mary B. Warren and Eve B. Weeks, *Whites Among the Cherokees* (Danielsville, GA, 1987).

1838: Laurens, Newton, and Tattnall County census originals are at the Archives and are also on microfilm. They are included in Brigid S. Townsend, *Indexes to Seven State Census Reports for Counties in Georgia, 1838-1845* (Atlanta, 1975). The original of the Lumpkin County census is incomplete but also at the Archives and on microfilm. It, too, is in Warren and Weeks, *Whites Among the Cherokees*. Paulding County's census is in the Telamon Cuyler Collection and is included in *Whites Among the Cherokees*. The statewide statistics for this census, by county, were published in the *Georgian*, Savannah, 18 and 19 December 1838.

1845: The Chatham, Dooly, Forsyth, and Warren County censuses are at the Archives and are also available on microfilm. Chatham County is included in *Censuses for Georgia Counties*, and Dooly, Forsyth, and Warren counties are included in Townsend's *Indexes to Seven State Census Reports*. The statistics for this census were published, by county, in George White's *Statistics of the State of Georgia* (New York, 1849).

1852: The Jasper County census and the census of the city of Augusta are at the Archives and are also available on microfilm. The latter was published by the Augusta Genealogical Society in *Ancestoring VI* (Augusta, 1983). The Chatham County census is still in the courthouse, though a microfilm copy is available at the Archives. The Morgan County census is at the courthouse and has never been microfilmed.

1853: The Morgan County census is at the courthouse and has never been microfilmed (not available at FHL).

1859: The Columbia County census is at the Archives and is also on microfilm. It was published by Merita Rozier, Leoda Sherry, and Nesba Wright, "State Census Columbia County, Georgia, 1859," *Georgia Genealogical Society Quarterly*, 13(1977):254. A census of wild lands in Terrell County is on microfilm at the Archives, while the original is still in the courthouse.

1865: Bulloch County's census is at the courthouse. It was published by Alvaretta K. Register, "1865 Census of Bulloch County, Georgia," *Georgia Genealogical Magazine*, no. 70 (1978):247.

1879: Columbia County (listed at FHL).

1890: A crude county copy of the lost federal census for Washington County is in the courthouse and on microfilm at the Archives.

There are also some censuses from the colonial period for a few counties that have been published in the *Georgia Genealogical Society Quarterly* (volumes 21, 24, 25, and 26). Some tax records from the 1850s and later at the Archives indicate the number of school children in each household and, starting in 1906, names and service of Confederate veterans are listed in county tax digests (a complete set of these tax digests beginning in 1872 is available at the Archives). The Georgia State Vital Records Unit had the originals of the state school census records for 1908, 1913, 1918, and 1923, but these records are now missing. County copies of some returns, however, are on microfilm at the Archives. These are for the counties of Fayette (1928, 1933, 1938), Henry (1903, 1908, 1913, 1918), Meriwether (1898, 1903, 1913), Tattnall (1928, 1933, 1938), and Walton (1928, 1933, 1938). Other school census records may still be in the counties.

Many thanks to Robert S. Davis, Jr., for his help with this section.

HAWAII

The censuses for 1878, 1890, and 1896 are located at:

Hawaii State Archives
Iolani Palace Grounds
Honolulu, Hawaii 96813

The 1878 census covers Oahu, Maui, and Hawaii and includes name, sex, age, marital status, nationality, and occupation. The 1890 census covers all the islands and includes name, sex, age, place of birth, marital status, mother of how many children and how many living, registered voter, and occupation. The 1896 census is for Honolulu only and includes name, sex, age, marital status, mother of how many children and how many living, nationality, citizenship status, registered voter, occupation, and religion.

The Source lists a compiled "census" for 1840-66, "compiled from school censuses, population schedules, tax lists, births and deaths; some in Hawaiian only. Original in state archives; microfilm at Genealogical Society of Utah." The FHL catalog also lists a microfilm of "census" material from 1847 to 1896. This consists of "school census statistics, population census statistics, and summaries of births, marriages, and deaths. Includes four pages of the original 1866 census of Hawaii, and loose sheets of corrections to a later (apparently the 1896) census of Hawaii."

ILLINOIS

The territorial censuses of 1810 and 1818 and state censuses for 1820, 1825, 1830, 1835, 1840, 1845, 1855, and 1865 are located at:

Illinois State Archives
Archives Building
Springfield, Illinois 62756

Territorial censuses were taken in 1810 (as Indiana Territory) and in 1818 (as Illinois Territory). Only Randolph County survives for 1810. These have been published in Margaret Cross Norton, *Illinois Census Returns 1810 and 1818* (1935, repr. Baltimore, 1969).

Like the pre-1850 federal censuses, the Illinois state censuses for 1820, 1825, 1830, 1835, 1840, and 1845 name only the head of household and list the rest of the members of the household in age categories. In 1820 and 1825, the age categories, although not uniform for all counties, generally included free white males twenty-one years of age and older; free white males under twenty-one; free white females; male and female servants and slaves; free persons of color. These censuses also recorded the type (e.g., mill, distillery) and number of manufacturing establishments. In 1830, 1835, 1840, and 1845, the age categories included white males and females in each decennial age group (e.g., age 0-9, 10-19, 20-29); male and female negroes and mulattoes, indentured or registered servants, and French negroes and mulattoes held in bondage. Also included were the total number of inhabitants in each household; number of males subject to duty in state militia; and type and number of manufacturing establishments. None of these censuses is complete for all the counties in the state; the following lists show what is extant for each county in each census year. (From Victoria Irons and Patricia C. Brennan, *Descriptive Inventory of the Archives of the State of Illinois* [Springfield, 1978], p. 34.)

1820:	Alexander	Jackson	Randolph
	Bond	Jefferson	St. Clair
	Clark	Johnson	Union
	Crawford	Madison	Washington
	Franklin	Monroe	Wayne
	Gallatin	Pope	White

This census has been published in Margaret Cross Norton, *Illinois Census Returns, 1820* (1934, repr. Baltimore, 1969).

1825: Edwards
Fulton
Randolph

1830: Morgan

1835: Fayette
Fulton
Jasper
Morgan
Putnam
Union

1840:

Adams	Effingham	Livingston
Bond	Franklin	Monroe
Brown	Fulton	Randolph
Calhoun	Hamilton	Rock Island
Champaign	Hardin	Schuyler
Clark	Jackson	Stark
Clay	Jasper	Tazewell
Clinton	Jo Daviess	Union
Coles	Johnson	Vermilion
Cook	Knox	White
Crawford	La Salle	Whiteside
Edgar	Lawrence	

1845: Cass
Madison
Montgomery
Putnam
Tazewell

1855: Names the head of household; "numbers of free white males and females in each decennial age group (e.g., ages 0-9, 10-19, 20-29); numbers of male and female Negroes and mulattoes; total number of inhabitants in household; number of males eligible for duty in state militia; type (e.g., mill, tinshop, saddleshop) and valuation of products of manufacturing establishments; valuations of livestock and products of coal mines; quantity (i.e., pounds) of wool produced; infrequent remarks (e.g., occupation of head of household, legal description of area covered by return). Also included in each return are numbers of colleges and common schools and number of pupils enrolled in each" (*Descriptive Inventory*, p. 36). The enumerations of five counties are missing: Franklin, Henry, Stark, Will, and Woodford, and only a summary (no names) exists for Carroll, Champaign, Gallatin, Jefferson, and Lake.

There is also an 1855 census of deaf and dumb, blind, and insane, but it is not indexed. "Entries for each individual include name, age, post office address, nature of ailment (i.e., deaf and dumb, blind, insane), name of head of family with whom residing" (*Descriptive Inventory*, p. 37). This is not available for all counties, and some counties (Greene, Grundy, McLean, Macoupin, Richland, Sangamon, and Whiteside) have this census attached to their returns for the 1855 state census.

1865: Names the head of household; "numbers of free white males and females in each decennial age group (e.g., age 0-9, 10-19, 20-29); numbers of male and female Negroes; total number of inhabitants in household; number of males eligible for duty in state militia; type (e.g., blacksmith shop, wheelwright shop) and valuation of products of manufacturing establishments; valuations of livestock, grain products, and other agricultural products; number and quantity (i.e., tons) of coal produced annually by coal mines; quantity (i.e., pounds) of wool products; numbers of flour and gristmills, sawmills, and distilleries. Also included in each return are numbers of universities, academies, grammar schools, and common schools, and number of pupils enrolled in each" (*Descriptive Inventory*, p. 38). This census is not fully indexed. Three counties are missing from this census: Gallatin, Mason, Monroe.

Genealogical Records and Mail Research Policy, a brochure available from the State Archives, says "1810-1855. The Archives has an index covering state and federal census records for this time span. We will search this index for two specifically named individuals, including both first and last names, for one census year in a designated county location." The Archives staff will also search the 1865 state census if a township location is provided.

Many thanks to Sandra Hargreaves Luebking for her help with this section.

INDIANA

The *Census of Indiana Territory for 1807* was published by the Indiana Historical Society (1980). It is a facsimile of the original manuscripts of Knox, Dearborn, and Randolph counties. The original for Clark County has not been found and in its place the Society used an 1807 voters list. They also added a poll list of Kaskaskia (Randolph County).

The Indiana Constitution of 1851 stipulated that an enumeration be made every six years of all the white male inhabitants over the age of twenty-one years. This requirement was first carried out in 1853 with each township assessor collecting the names of white male inhabitants and filing the list with the county auditor. In 1865 the prodedure was modified to include the age of each white male and in 1877 the law was amended to include a separate list of negro males over the age of twenty-one years. The revised edition of *Ancestry's Red Book*, after citing the 1807 territorial census, says "No other state censuses exist, although state enumerations of males (without names) above age twenty-one were taken at various intervals beginning in 1820." This may be true for some counties, but the 1853 census for Hendricks and Jennings counties, available at the FHL, clearly lists the names of every white male over twenty-one.

These state censuses are not complete for every county and except for Hendricks and Jennings counties in 1853, they are not available at the FHL. Some original censuses are located at:

> Indiana State Library
> 140 North Senate Avenue
> Indianapolis, Indiana 46204

The State Library has the following censuses:

1857: Hartford City, Blackford County
1871: Scattered townships, Blackford County
1877: Scattered townships, Blackford County
    Five townships of Fayette County
1883: Scattered townships, Blackford County
1889: Scattered townships, Blackford County
1901: Jackson township, Washington County
1913: Henry County
1919: Jackson township, Ripley County
    Center township, Starke County
1931: Henry County

A series was produced in 1940 by the Indiana Historical Records Survey called the *Inventory of the County Archives of Indiana.* Each county was given a volume, though not all counties were completed. This is probably the best source for determining which state censuses still exist for your county of interest.

IOWA

The state censuses are located at:

State Historical Society of Iowa
The Historical Division of the Department of Cultural Affairs
600 E. Locust, Capitol Complex
Des Moines, Iowa 50319

Iowa took the following territorial and state censuses:

1836: Taken as part of the Wisconsin Territorial Census; exists only for Dubuque and Des Moines counties. Lists the head of household and the number of males and females within certain age brackets.

1838: Cedar, Clayton, Clinton, Johnson, Lee, Louisa, Muscatine, Slaughter, and Van Buren counties. Lists names of masters, mistresses, stewards, overseers or other principal persons; white males, white females, free males of color, and free females of color. Only Van Buren County is available at the FHL.

1844: Only Keokuk County. Lists the head of household and the number of males over 21, males under 21, and females.

1846: Louisa, Polk, and Wapello counties. Lists the head of household and the number of males under 21, males over 21, females under 21, and females over 21.

1847: Clinton, Davis, Louisa, Marion, Scott, Wapello, and Van Buren counties. Lists the head of household and the total number of persons living in the household.

1849: Benton, Boone, Clinton, Jackson, Louisa, Madison, Poweshiek, Scott, Van Buren, and Washington counties.

1851: Cedar, Clinton, Decatur, Guthrie, Iowa, Johnson, Madison, Mahaska, Page, Pottawattamie, Poweshiek, Scott, and Washington counties.

1852: Manuscript schedules are extant for thirty-nine counties and abstracts of data for eight counties.

1854: Manuscript schedules are extant for fifty counties and abstracts of data for fourteen counties.

1856: Lists the members of the household and all others living in the household. Gives the number of years a person has been in the state of Iowa.

1885: Lists the members of the household and all others living in the household. County of birth is given if born in Iowa.

1895: Lists the members of the household and all others living in the household. This also gives the company, regiment (infantry or cavalry) and state for Civil War service. County of birth is given if born in Iowa.

1905: Lists the members of the household, place of birth of father and mother, occupation, war service, number of years in Iowa and U.S. if foreign born.

1915: Lists name, age, county, town or township, occupation, total earnings, extent of education, place of birth, military service, church affiliation, father's and mother's birthplace, if foreign born, if naturalized, years in Iowa and U.S., sex, color, marital status, months in school in 1914, read, write, blind, deaf, insane or idiot.

1925: Lists names, place of abode, relationship to head of household, citizenship, education, names of parents (including mother's maiden name), nativity of parents, place of marriage of parents, military service, occupation and religion. There is a separate index.

The State Historical Society has an "Application for Census Search" which says they will search a town or township, though not a whole county. No more than two census requests can be made at one time. They charge $5.00 (non-refundable) for the first half-hour of searching, and $3.00 for each additional half-hour.

Many of the early state censuses have been published in *Hawkeye Heritage*:

> 1849 Boone County Census, 1(1966):5
> 1838 Van Buren County Census, 1(1966):6
> The 1847 Iowa Census - Van Buren County, 1(1966):10
> 1836 Census of Dubuque County, 1(1966):60
> 1836 Census of Demoine County, 1(1966):91
> 1852 Census, Appanoose County, 2(1967):13
> 1846 Census, Wapello County, 2(1967):32
> Index, 1847 Census Wapello County, 2(1967):39

1853 Census Warren County, 2(1967):81
1854 Special Census, Dallas County, 2(1967):138
Kossuth County, 1856 State Census, 3(1968):43
1847 Special Census, Marion County, 3(1968):60
Hardin County, 1856 State Census, 3(1968):108
Special Census, Clarke County, 3(1968):160
1854 Special Census, Henry County, 4(1969):108
1836 Census of Demoine County, The T's, U's & V's, 5(1970):7
1856 State Census, Calhoun County, 5(1970):157
Census of 1854, Story County, Heads of Families, 6(1971):144
Iowa Territorial Census 1846, Louisa County, 9(1974):109
Iowa State Census 1847, Clinton County, 10(1975):114
1844 Census of Iowa Territory, Keokuk County, 10(1975):175
1847 State Census, Davis County, 11(1976):18
Index to the 1856 Census of Story County, 13(1978):167
Index to the 1856 Special State Census of Franklin County, 22(1987):136
1854 Special Census of Wayne County, 23(1988):155
1885 Census, College for the Blind, Vinton, Benton County, 24(1989):30
1895 State Census of Iowa Soldiers Home, Marshalltown, Marshall County, 23(1988):205
1895 Census, St. Francis Convent, Dubuque City, Ward 5, Dubuque County, 24(1989):26
1895 Census, St. Mary's Orphan Home, Dubuque City, Ward 5, Dubuque County, 24(1989):27

And a few have been published in *The American Genealogist*:

1844 Census of Iowa Territory, Keokuk County, 42(1966):136
Iowa Territorial Census 1846, Louisa County, 43(1967):111
1847 Iowa State Census, Davis County, 42(1966):232
Iowa State Census 1847, Clinton County, 43(1967):59

KANSAS

The original and microfilm copies of the state censuses are located at:

Newspaper and Census Division
Kansas State Historical Society
120 W. 10th
Topeka, Kansas 66612

If the microfilm of the state census cannot be read, the original copy can be requested, but since the originals are housed off-site by the Historical Society, it might take some time. Interlibrary loan of microfilms is also available; write to the Microfilm Loan Department at the above address for further information.

A brochure, *Information Contained in the Kansas Census Records*, is available from the State Historical Society. Kansas took the following state censuses:

1855: A list of eligible voters, rather than a state census, with ages given by deciles. Some entries list names of family members, some give the number only. This census has been indexed by Accelerated Indexing Systems.

1860: A territorial census taken as part of the 1860 federal census. The state copy has been indexed and is available at the Kansas State Historical Society.

1865: Lists all in the household by name, and gives age, sex, race or color, and state or country of birth; and in addition marital status and military record (company and regiment).

1875: Lists all in the household by name, and gives age, sex, race or color, and state or country of birth; and in addition where from to Kansas (state or country).

1885: Lists all in the household by name, and gives age, sex, race or color, marital status, occupation of those over 10 and the trade or profession being learned by those under 21, and state or country of birth; and in addition where from to Kansas (state or country) and military record (condition of discharge, state of enlistment, letter or name of company or command, number of regiment or other organization to which attached, arm of the service, and name of prison if confined to one).

This census also has an agricultural schedule which is quite detailed. It asks general questions about the size and cultivation of the farm and then asks about crops (including listings for four different kinds of corn), gardens, dairy products, livestock (including the number who died of disease and the number killed by dogs and wolves), orchards, vineyards, bees, and dogs.

1895:   Same as 1885; this census also has an agricultural schedule as in 1885.

1905:   Same as 1885, but drops marital status.

1915:   Same as 1885, but drops marital status; also has a column asking for home libraries of more than twenty volumes.

1925: Same as 1885; and in addition relationship to head of house, marital status and citizenship (year of immigration to U.S. and year of naturalization if naturalized). This is not available at the FHL.

The 1855 and 1865 state censuses are indexed, and an index is presently being compiled for 1885. All others are unindexed and filed by county, township and/or city.

Many thanks to Rowena Horr for her help with this section.

KENTUCKY

Kentucky did not take any state censuses. The General Assembly did require school censuses to be taken beginning in 1888 and going into the early 1900s. These may include the name, parents, residence, age, and birth date for those individuals who attended public school. But these school censuses, where they still exist, may be found only in the local boards of education. They may also not be open to the public but only available to the person listed. A few of these school records and also tax lists (which can be helpful for finding adult males) are available at:

Kentucky State Archives
Department of Libraries and Archives
300 Coffee Tree Road
P.O. Box 537
Frankfort, Kentucky 40602

Kentucky Historical Society
P.O. Box H
Frankfort, Kentucky 40602-2108

The following published books based on tax lists may also be of help:

Charles B. Heinemann, *First Census of Kentucky, 1790* (1940, repr. Baltimore, 1965).
G. Glenn Clift, *Second Census of Kentucky, 1800* (1954, repr. Baltimore, 1966).
James F. Sutherland, *Early Kentucky Householders 1781-1811* (Baltimore, 1986).
James F. Sutherland, *Early Kentucky Landholders 1787-1811* (Baltimore, 1986).

Many thanks to Dr. Roseann R. Hogan for her help with this section.

LOUISIANA

There are 1791 and 1804 censuses of New Orleans and 1849-1864 New Orleans registers of free persons of color available at:

Louisiana State Archives
3851 Essen Lane
P.O. Box 94125
Baton Rouge, Louisiana 70804

The FHL catalog lists an 1856/7 census for Carrollton and an 1870 census for Assumption Parish.

A few early French and Spanish censuses have been published:

Bill Barron, *Census of Pointe Coupee, Louisiana, 1745* (New Orleans, 1978).

Roscoe R. Hill, *Descriptive Catalogue of the Documents Relating to the History of the United States in the Papeles Procedentes de Cuba Deposited in the Archivo General de Indias* (1916, repr. New York, 1965).

Charles R. Maduell, Jr., *The Census Tables for the French Colony of Louisiana from 1699 through 1732* (Baltimore, 1972).

Elizabeth Shown Mills, *Natchitoches Colonials: Censuses, Military Rolls, and Tax Lists 1722-1803.* Vol. 5, Cane River Creole Series (Chicago, 1981).

Jacqueline K. Voorhies, *Some Late Eighteenth Century Louisianians, 1758-1796* (Lafayette, La., 1973).

MAINE

On 23 June 1836 the United States Congress voted to apportion a surplus of money collected from tariffs and the sale of public lands among the several states. The Maine legislature voted on 26 January 1837 to accept its portion of the surplus. Towns were to vote to receive their share after taking a census. This census is called the Surplus Revenue Census of 1837, or the 1837 State Census.

This census was to include those residing in the household on 1 March 1837 except unnaturalized foreigners whose residence had not been established for at least four years and untaxed Indians. The families were generally enumerated under the name of the head of household and then by age categories for those under 4, those 4 to 21, and those over 21; totals for each family were in the fourth column.

The original censuses of Bangor (seven wards), Portland (seven wards), and all the then unorganized towns, townships, and plantations (see list at end of section) are located at:

> The Maine State Archives
> State House Station 84
> Augusta, Maine 04333

The original census for Eliot, Maine, is located at:

> The Maine Historical Society
> 485 Congress Street
> Portland, Maine 04101

On 30 April 1838 the town of Eliot voted to divide the balance of the surplus among the inhabitants with each individual in town to receive $1.91. Therefore, every person in town was enumerated by name and age, and in some cases by relationship to head of household, i.e. "wife of," "children of," "mother of." This census was organized by school district and is sometimes referred to as the "Eliot School Surplus Tax."

The 1837 census for two towns have been published:

> Alice MacDonald Long, "Town of Mount Desert, Census of 1837, John Manchester Jr., Enumerator," *The Maine Seine*, 11(1989):44.

Thomas H. Roderick and Alice MacDonald Long, "The 1837 Maine Census: Gray Surplus and 80 Rod Strip, Cumberland County," *The Maine Seine*, 12(1990):35.

The following are the towns and unorganized townships and plantations for which the Maine State Archives have the original 1837 census. The counties in which they were then located are also noted. The question marks appear on the list supplied by the State Archives. In parentheses are the township (T) and range (R) designations.

Adamstown (T4 R2), Oxford Co.
Andover North Surplus, Oxford Co.
Aroostook River, along the, Washington Co.
Ashland (T11 R5 WELS), Penobscot Co.
Bangor (7 wards), Penobscot Co.
Benedicta (T2 R5 WELS Catholic Township), Penobscot Co.
Between the Piscataquis River and the west branch of the Penobscot River, Penobscot Co.
Bowtown (T1 R4 WKR), Somerset Co.
Bradford (T1 R5), Penobscot Co.
Bridgewater (Bridgewater Academy Grant), Washington Co.
Brookton Township (T9 R3), Washington Co.
Burnham (annexed part of Clinton Gore), Kennebec Co.
Carrabasset Valley (T3 R2 WKR), Somerset Co.
Carratunk Plantation (T1 R3 EKR), Somerset Co.
Carroll Plantation (T6 R2), Penobscot Co.
Cary Plantation (T11 R1), Washington Co.
Clifton (Jarvis Gore), Penobscot Co.
Clinton (annexed part of Clinton Gore), Kennebec Co.
Coplin Plantation, Oxford Co.
Dallas (T2 R2), Oxford Co.
Danforth (Danforth's half township), Washington Co.
Dead River (T3 R3 WKR BKP), Somerset Co.
Denmark (part of Fryeburg Academy Grant), Oxford Co.
Dennistown (T5 R2 state land), Somerset Co.
Dennysville, Washington Co.
Drew Plantation (T7 R4), Penobscot Co.
Dyer (T1 R2), Washington Co.
Eaton (T9 R4), Washington Co.
Eustis (Bath Academy Grant), Oxford Co.
Flagstaff (T4 R4 WKR BKP), Somerset Co.
Forest City (T9 R4), Washington Co.
Forks, The (T1 R4 EKR), Somerset Co.

Fowler (part of Dyer Township T1 R2), Washington Co.
Garland (part of Williams College Grant), Washington Co.
Grafton (TA No. 2), Oxford Co.
Greenbush (Upper East Indian Township?), Penobscot Co.
Gray Surplus, see Raymond
Haynesville (Dole Township 9), Washington Co.
Highland Plantation (T2 R2 WKR BP), Somerset Co.
Hopkins Academy Grants, East and West (near Millinocket),
    Penobscot Co.
Jackman (T4 R1, state land), Somerset Co.
Lakeville Plantation (T4 R1), Penobscot Co.
Lincoln Plantation (T5 R2), Oxford Co.
Littleton (part of Williams College), Washington Co.
Ludlow (Belfast Academy Grant), Washington Co.
Magalloway (T5 R1), Oxford Co.
Mapleton (T12 R3 WELS), Penobscot Co.
Masardis (T10 R5 WELS), Penobscot Co.
Mason (Part of Fryeburg Academy Grant), Oxford Co.
Matinicus, Lincoln Co.
Mattawamkeag (Lower East Township?, Lower West Indian
    Township #2?), Penobscot Co.
Medway (TA R6), Penobscot Co.
Monhegan, Lincoln Co.
Moose River (T4 R2 state land), Somerset Co.
Mount Chase Plantation (T5 R6 WELS), Penobscot Co.
Muscle Ledge Islands, Lincoln Co.
New Gloucester (annexed part of the Eighty-Rod Strip), Cumber-
    land Co.
Oakfield (T5 R3 WELS), Penobscot Co.
Orient (Orient Gore), Washington Co.
Osborn Plantation (21 BP), Hancock Co.
Parlin Pond (T3 R7 WKR BKP), Somerset Co.
Passadumkeag (Lower East Indian Township #1?), Penobscot Co.
Patten (T4 R6 WELS), Penobscot Co.
Plantation 14, Washington Co.
Plantation 17, Washington Co.
Plantation 18, Washington Co.
Plantation 19, Washington Co.
Plantation 24, Washington Co.
Plantation 29, Washington Co.
Pleasant Ridge Plantation, Somerset Co.
Poland, Cumberland Co.
Portland (7 wards and off shore islands), Cumberland Co.

Rangeley, town of (T3 R2), Oxford Co.

Raymond (annexed parts of Gray Surplus, Eighty-Rod Strip, the Cape), Cumberland Co.

Reed (T1 R3 WELS), Penobscot Co.

Richardsontown (T4 R1), Oxford Co.

Riley (TA No. 1), Oxford Co.

Sandy Bay (T5 R3 Sandy Bay Co.), Somerset Co.

Sherman (T3 R5 WELS), Penobscot Co.

Silver Ridge Township (T2 RS WELS Catholic Township), Penobscot Co.

Smyrna (T6 R3 WELS), Penobscot Co.

Standish (The Cape), Cumberland Co.

Stoneham (part of Fryeburg Academy Grant), Oxford Co.

Talmadge (T3 R2), Washington Co.

Topsfield (T8 R2), Washington Co.

Township A R2, Washington Co.

Township A R7, Penobscot Co.

Township C, Oxford Co.

Township E, Oxford Co.

Township 1 R3 WKR, Somerset Co.

Township 1 R5 WELS, Penobscot Co.

Township 2R WELS, Penobscot Co.

Township 3 R1 NBPP, Penobscot Co.

Township 3 R1, Washington Co.

Township 3 R7 WELS, Penobscot Co.

Township 7 R5 WELS, Penobscot Co.

Township 11 R3 NBPP, Washington Co.

Unity Plantation (plantation north of Albion), Kennebec Co.

Upton (Tp. B), Oxford Co.

Waite (T2 R2), Washington Co.

Washburn (T13 R3 WELS), Penobscot Co.

West Forks Plantation (T1 R5 WKR BKP), Somerset Co.

Weston (Monroe Gore), Washington Co.

Willimantic (T8 R8 NWP), Somerset Co.

Winn (River T4 R3), Penobscot Co.

Woodstock (T2 now a part of), Oxford Co.

Woodville (Lower West Indian Township #2?), Penobscot Co.

Wyman (T4 R3 WKR), Somerset Co.

Many thanks to Lois Ware Thurston for her help with this section.

MARYLAND

Maryland did not take any censuses after statehood, but in 1776 a census of the population was taken. For most areas this census lists the head of household and the rest of the people in each household in age categories of males under 16, males from 16 to 50, males above 50, females under 16, females from 16 to 50, and females above 50. But a few of the enumerators listed all members of the household with their ages, and a few even listed the names and ages of the blacks in each household.

This census has been published twice, first by Gaius Marcus Brumbaugh in *Maryland Records, Colonial, Revolutionary, County and Church from Original Sources*, 2 vols. (1915-28; repr. Baltimore, 1967), and then by Bettie Stirling Carothers in *1776 Census of Maryland* (1972). Most of the records have been transcribed, but for some hundreds, as indicated below, Brumbaugh published facsimile reproductions of the original pages:

Anne Arundel County: All Hallows Parish
　　　　　　　　　　　Head of household and age categories
　　　　　　　　　　　Facsimile reproduction
　　　　　　　　　　St. James Parish
　　　　　　　　　　　Head of household and age categories
　　　　　　　　　　　Facsimile reproduction

Caroline County:　　　Bredge Town Hundred
　　　　　　　　　　　Head of household and age categories
　　　　　　　　　　　Transcribed

Dorchester County:　　Nantacoake Hundred
　　　　　　　　　　　Head of household and age categories
　　　　　　　　　　　Transcribed
　　　　　　　　　　Straight's Hundred
　　　　　　　　　　　Head of household and age categories
　　　　　　　　　　　Transcribed
　　　　　　　　　　Transquakin Hundred
　　　　　　　　　　　Head of household and age categories
　　　　　　　　　　　Transcribed

Frederick County:　　Lower Potomac Hundred
　　　　　　　　　　　Males and females in separate alphabetical
　　　　　　　　　　　　lists with ages
　　　　　　　　　　　Transcribed
　　　　　　　　　　George Town Hundred

Males and females in separate alphabetical
lists with ages
Transcribed
Unnamed Hundred (now Montgomery
County)
Names everyone with ages, includes blacks
Transcribed
Elizabeth Hundred
Males and females in separate age category
lists
Facsimile reprodution
Sugar Land Hundred
Names everyone with ages, includes blacks
Transcribed
North West Hundred
Names everyone with ages, includes blacks
Transcribed

Harford County: Broad Creek Hundred
Names everyone with ages
Transcribed
Bush River Lower Hundred
Names everyone with ages, includes blacks
Facsimile reproduction
Specutia Lower Hundred
Names everyone with ages, includes blacks
Facsimile reproduction
Deer Creek Lower Hundred
Names everyone with ages, includes blacks
Transcribed
Harford Lower Hundred
Names everyone with ages, includes some
blacks
Transcribed
Susquehannah Hundred
Names everyone with ages, includes some
blacks
Transcribed

Prince George's County: St. John and Prince George's Parishes
Names everyone with ages, includes some
blacks
Facsimile reproduction

Queen Anne's County: Town Hundred
    Head of household and age categories
    Transcribed
Upper Hundred, Kent Island
    Head of household and age categories
    Transcribed
Wye Hundred
    Head of household and age categories
    Facsimile reproduction

Talbott County: Bay Hundred
    Head of household and age categories
    Transcribed
Mill Hundred
    Head of household and age categories
    Transcribed
Tuckahoe Hundred
    Head of household and age categories
    Transcribed

In the original census, some of the enumerators listed the males in the household in descending order of age followed by the females in descending order of age. Brumbaugh (and therefore Carothers, who seems to have copied Brumbaugh) moved the females with the same surname as the males into a position just after these males. In most cases they were probably a family, but this assumption may be incorrect. The following example supplied by Gordon Remington shows how one family was listed in the original census and how they are then listed in Brumbaugh and Carothers:

Original	Brumbaugh and Carothers
George Willson, age 30	George Willson
William Wilson, age 8	William Willson
Michel Wilson, age 6	Michel Willson
George Wilson, age 4	George Willson
Joseph Hools, age 37	Lidia Willson
Benjamin Shaw, age 13	Elizabeth Willson
John Hibbey/Kibby, age 8	Joseph Hools
Elisabeth Robey, age 56	Benjamin Shaw
Lidia Wilson, age 26	John Hibbey
Dorraty Shaw, age 20	Elizabeth Robey
Elisabeth Wilson, age 1	Dorraty Shaw

Brumbaugh also includes a Constable's Census of Charles County, 1775-1778. This lists male persons eighteen years and upward in the Lower Hundred, Benedict Hundred, Port Tobacco West Hundred, Upper Hundred, East Hundred, Port Tobacco Upper Hundred, Port Tobacco Town Hundred, Port Tobacco East Hundred, Pomonkey Hundred, Newport West Hundred, William and Mary Lower Hundred, and Bryan Town Hundred.

Many thanks to Gordon Remington for his help with this section.

MASSACHUSETTS

Originals and microfilm copies of the state censuses are located at:

Massachusetts State Archives
Columbia Point
220 Morrissey Blvd.
Boston, Massachusetts 02125

Massachusetts took state censuses every ten years from 1855 to 1945, but original population returns exist only for 1855 and 1865. There are published summaries for these two years and the later years, for which see Henry J. Dubester, *State Censuses, An Annotated Bibliography of Censuses of Population Taken After the Year 1790 by States and Territories of the United States* (Washington, D.C., 1948).

1855: Names all members of the household; age; sex; color; occupation; place of birth (generally state or country); and whether a person was deaf, dumb, blind, insane, idiotic, pauper, or convict.

1865: Names all members of the household; age; sex; color; place of birth (generally state or country); marital status (married, widowed, or single); occupation; whether a person was deaf, dumb, blind, insane, idiotic, pauper, or convict; and whether a man was a ratable poll (over the age of 16 and owns enough property to be taxed), a legal voter, or a naturalized voter.

These two censuses are currently being published town by town. Each volume contains both the 1855 and 1865 censuses for the town, transcribed in original order, followed by an index of heads of household and persons of other surnames in the household. For a brochure of available towns and their prices, send a business size SASE to: Ann S. Lainhart, P.O. Box 1487, Boston, Massachusetts 02117.

As of the date of this publication seventy-one towns have been completed; in some cases two towns have been put into a single volume:

Essex County:
North Andover
Boxford & West Boxford
Bradford
Essex
Georgetown
Middleton & Nahant
Newbury
West Newbury
Rockport
Saugus

Groveland & Hamilton   Swampscott
Ipswich   Topsfield
Lynnfield & Manchester Wenham

Middlesex County:

Acton   Natick
Bedford   South Reading
Billerica   Sherborn
Boxborough & Brighton   Shirley
  & Burlington   Stoneham
Charlestown (2 vols.)   Stow
Chelmsford   Sudbury
Concord   Tewksbury
Dracut & Dunstable   Townsend &
Groton   Tyngsborough
Holliston   Watertown
Hopkinton   Wayland
Lexington   West Cambridge
Lincoln & Littleton   Westford
Marlborough   Weston
Medford   Wilmington
Melrose   Winchester

Plymouth County:

Bridgewater   Hingham
East Bridgewater   Marshfield
North Bridgewater   Middleborough
West Bridgewater   Pembroke
Duxbury   Plympton
Halifax & Hull   Rochester
Hanover   Wareham
Hanson

Meta L. Stark is publishing the 1855 census for Berkshire county towns in the *Berkshire Genealogist* and has completed the following towns:

Becket, 4(1983):86
North Becket, 6(1985):81
Cheshire, 7(1986):43
Tyringham, 9(1988):92
Mt. Washington, 10(1989):52
Clarksburg, 10(1989):85
New Ashford, 10(1989):125
Alford, 11(1990):25
Florida, 11(1990):117
Hancock, 12(1991):96

One of the unusual features of the Massachusetts state censuses is that the enumerators in several towns entered specific town of birth instead of just state or country. In some cases this is only for those born in Massachusetts or in the United States, but in other towns it may include county, parish, or town of birth in other countries. Also it may only be one enumerator out of two or three within a particular town that did this. A list follows of the twenty-two towns in 1855 and the ninety-six towns in 1865 with this feature; those with an asterisk (*) are published:

	1855	1865
Barnstable County:	Dennis	Chatham
	Harwich	Dennis
	Provincetown	Falmouth
	Wellfleet	Harwich
	Yarmouth	Wellfleet
		Yarmouth
Berkshire County:	New Ashford	Cheshire
		Florida
		Hancock
		Lee
		Lenox
		Monterey
		New Ashford
Bristol County:	Marshfield	Dartmouth
	North Attleboro	Freetown
	Westport	New Bedford - Ward 4
		Rehoboth
		Somerset
Dukes County:		Edgartown
		Gosnold
		Tisbury
Essex County:	Andover	Essex*
	Ipswich*	Ipswich*
		Lynn - Wards 3, 4, 5
		Lynnfield*
		Middleton*
		Rockport*
		South Danvers
		Swampscott*

	1855	1865
Franklin County:	Shutesbury	Ashfield
		Gill
		Hawley
		Leyden
		Monroe
		New Salem
		Northfield
		Shutesbury
		Wendell
Hampden County:	Brimfield	Brimfield
	Holland	Chester
		Holland
		Monson
		Palmer
		Russell
Hampshire County:	Enfield	Cummington
		Greenwich
		Hadley
		Ware
		Williamsburg
Middlesex County:	Carlisle	Bedford*
	Wayland*	Boxborough*
	Wilmington*	Carlisle
		Charlestown*
		Dunstable*
		Framingham
		Groton*
		Hopkinton*
		Lexington*
		Littleton*
		Marlborough*
		Melrose*
		North Reading
		Pepperell
		Reading
		Sherborn*
		Watertown*
		Wayland*
		Westford*
		Wilmington*

1855	1865
Norfolk County:Brookline	Brookline
	Dorchester
	Foxborough
	Milton
	Needham
	Quincy
	Sharon
	Stoughton
	Weymouth
Plymouth County: Abington	Halifax*
Pembroke*	Marshfield*
	North Bridgewater*
	Rochester*
	Scituate*
	Wareham*
Suffolk County:	Winthrop
Worcester County:	Ashburnham
	Berlin
	Bolton
	Boylston
	Grafton
	Leicester
	Lunenburg
	Sutton
	Uxbridge
	Westborough
	Westminster

MICHIGAN

Original and microfilm copies of the state censuses are available at:

State Archives
Michigan Department of State
717 W. Allegan Street
Lansing, MI 48918-1837

For background researchers may wish to read "State Censuses of Michigan, A Tragedy of Lost Treasures," *Family Trails*, 6(1978), or Donna Valley Russell, *Michigan Censuses 1710-1830 Under the French, British, and Americans* (Detroit, 1982). The first volume is available from the Genealogy Section, Library of Michigan, P.O. Box 30007, Lansing, Michigan 48909.

Michigan took the following state censuses:

1837: Does not include individual names but gives the number of males and females; number of deaf and dumb; those under 10; those of 10 and under 21; those of 21 and under 45; those of 45 and under 75; and those over 75; and the number of colored persons. The FHL has only Kalamazoo County.

1845: Same as 1837 with addition of the names of all males over 21 years of age and the number of insane. This census has been published in Ronald Vern Jackson, *Michigan 1845 State Census* (AIS) and includes the counties of St. Joseph, Lenawee, Washtenaw, and Eaton.

1854: Name, profession, and marital status of all males over 21; the number of females in age categories (distinguishing the married from the unmarried); the number of children under 21 (distinguishing the males from the females); the number of deaf, dumb, blind, and insane; the number of marriages and deaths in the preceding year. Also has agricultural and industrial schedules. Statistical abstract published by the Secretary of State: *Census and Statistics of the State of Michigan, 1854.* The FHL has only Eaton County.

1864: Same as 1854. Statistical abstract published by the Secretary of State: *Census and Statistics of the State of Michigan, 1864.* The FHL has only the counties of Eaton, Clinton, Houghton, and St. Joseph (Leonides township).

1874: Same as 1854. Statistical abstract published by the Secretary of State: *Census of the State of Michigan, 1874*. The FHL has only the counties of Eaton and Houghton.

1884: Names each member of the household, age, sex, color, place of birth (state or country of each citizen and his or her parents), occupation, marital status, physical and mental condition, literacy, and length of residence in Michigan. Also has mortality, agricultural, and industrial schedules. Statistical abstract published by the Secretary of State: *Census of the State of Michigan, 1884*. The FHL does not have the counties of Hillsdale, Jackson, Muskegon, Newaygo, Roscommon, St. Clair, and St. Joseph.

1888: A special Civil War veterans census was taken.

1894: Same as 1884 with the addition of number of months employed during the census year; number of years resided in the United States; whether a prisoner, convict, homeless child, or pauper; if a Civil War veteran or widow of same. Statistical abstract published by the Secretary of State: *Census of the State of Michigan, 1894*. Also see *United States Civil War Soldiers Living in Michigan in 1894*, prepared by the Genealogists of the Clinton County Historical Society, St. Johns, Michigan in 1988. The FHL does not have the counties of Hillsdale, Midland, St. Clair, and St. Joseph.

1904: A three card system was used: a yellow card for each family listing head of household, address, and number of persons of each sex in the family. A blue card for each male and a red card for each female listing name, address, relation to head of household, physical characteristics, race, age, conjugal condition, voting status, native or foreign born, literacy, ability to speak English, school attendance, place of birth of parents, number of years of residence in Michigan and United States. Unfortunately, this census has been completely destroyed and only the statistical abstract published by the Secretary of State still exists: *Census of the State of Michigan, 1904*.

Not all of the above censuses are available for each county in each year, and in some cases only part of a county may still exist. The following chart lists the censuses available at the State Archives by year, the type of census schedule (Inhabitants, Mortality, Agriculture, Industry, Social Statistics*), and whether there is an index:

County	Year	Inhabit.	Mortal.	Agricul.	Industry	Social	Index
Allegan	1894			X			
Barry	1884	X	X	X	X		
	1894	X	X		X	X	
Bay	1884	X	X	X	X		
	1894	X	X	X	X	X	
Benzie	1884	X					
	1894	X					
Clinton	1864	X		X	X		
Dickinson	1894	X	X				
Eaton	1845	X					X
	1854	X		X	X		X
	1864	X		X	X		
	1874	X		X	X		
Emmet	1884	X			X	X	X
	1894		X	X	X		
Gratiot	1894	X					
Hillsdale	1884	X					
	1894	X					
Houghton	1864	X					
	1874	X					
Ingham	1884	X	X	X	X	X	
	1894	X		X	X		
Iosco	1894	X					
Isabella	1884		X		X		
	1894				X		
Jackson	1884	X					
	1894	X					
Kalamazoo	1884	X					
	1894	X					
Kent	1884	X	X	X	X		
	1894	X		X			
Keweenaw	1884	X	X	X	X		
	1894	X		X	X		
Lake	1934	X					
Lapeer	1884	X					
	1894	X					
Menominee	1884	X		X	X		
	1894	X	X	X			
Midland	1894	X					
Montcalm	1884	X			X	X	X
	1894	X					

County	Year	Inhabit.	Mortal.	Agricul.	Industry	Social	Index
Muskegon	1884	X	X			X	
	1894	X	X			X	
Newaygo	1864	X		X	X		
	1884	X	X	X	X	X	X
	1894	X					
Ottawa	1884	X					
	1894	X		X			
Roscommon	1884	X		X	X		
St. Clair	1884	X					
	1894	X					
St. Joseph	1845	X					X
	1884	X			X	X	
	1894	X			X	X	
Van Buren	1845	X					
Wexford	1884					X	

*Social Statistics include information about:
1. Schools: number of teachers and their wages, number of pupils, value of estate, kind and amount of taxes, number of months in session, and type of building construction.
2. Libraries: name of or indentification of owner and number of volumes.
3. Churches: name, denomination, ownership of parsonage, type of construction material, seating capacity, and value of property.
4. Newspapers: name, frequency, and circulation.

The FHL catalog also lists Washtenaw County with 1884 and 1894 censuses including the population, agricultural, industrial, and social schedules.

A few early French and English censuses were taken for Detroit and these and some of the above state censuses have been published:

Donna Valley Stuart, "Detroit 1762 Census," *National Genealogical Society Quarterly*, 68(1980):15.

Donna Valley Stuart, "1765 Census of Detroit, Wayne County, Michigan, *Detroit Society for Genealogical Research Magazine*, 43(1979):19.

Donna Valley Stuart, "Detroit 1796 Census," *National Genealogical Society Quarterly*, 69(1981):185.

Mrs. Edgar M. Montgomery and Mrs. Raymond Millbrook, "Wayne County Returns from the Michigan Territorial Census of 1827," *Detroit Society for Genealogical Research Magazine*, 19(1955):51.

Ruth Robbins Monteith and Ethel W. Williams, "Michigan State Census of Kalamazoo County, 1837," *Michigan Heritage*, 1(1959):70.

Census Records of Lenawee County, Michigan Territory, 1845, typescript at the State Library, includes areas now in Hillsdale County.

Betty Williams, *1845 State Census, St. Joseph County, Michigan* (Kalamazoo, 1968).

The 1884 state census for the townships of Greenfield, Dearborn, Livonia, Huron, and Ecorse, Wayne County, have appeared in the *Detroit Society for Genealogical Research Magazine* beginning with volume 44.

Eva Harmison-Arnold, "1894 State Census of Dickinson County, Michigan," *Detroit Society for Genealogical Research Magazine*, 42(1978):11.

Genealogical Society of Washtenow County, *Index of 1894 State Census for Washtenow Co., Michigan* (1984).

Many thanks to LeRoy Barnett for his help on this Michigan section.

MINNESOTA

Original and microfilm copies of all the territorial and state censuses are located at:

Minnesota Historical Society
Minnesota History Center
345 Kellogg Boulevard West
St. Paul, Minnesota 55102-1906

The original copies of these censuses are closed to public use.

The Minnesota Historical Society has published *Genealogical Resources of the Minnesota Historical Society, A Guide* (St. Paul, 1989) which contains information on all the territorial, state, and federal censuses. This publication is available from the Society.

The earliest census listings for the area that later became Minnesota are found in the 1820 Michigan territorial census. The 1830 territorial censuses do not seem to include Minnesota. The 1836 Wisconsin territorial census, however, may include portions of present-day Minnesota as part of Crawford County and as part of Dubuque County (later in Iowa Territory). Portions of Minnesota are also in the 1838 Wisconsin Territory census as part of Crawford and Clayton counties. Minnesota inhabitants are included in the 1840 Wisconsin and Iowa territorial censuses.

The Minnesota Historical Society has microfilm copies of the 1836, 1838, and 1840 Wisconsin and the 1840 Iowa territorial censuses.

Minnesota took the following territorial and state censuses:

1849: Name of head of household; number of males; number of females. Published in Minnesota (Territory), Legislative Assembly, *Journal of the House of Representatives, First Session of the Territory of Minnesota*, 1850, Appendices C and D, pp. 195-215. This census has been indexed by Ronald Vern Jackson, *Minnesota 1849 Census Index* (AIS, 1981).

1853: Name of head of household; number of children; number in household; names of inhabitants (for some communities only). The returns are very incomplete. This census is in manuscript form only and is not available through interlibrary loan. This is not available at the FHL.

1855: Name of head of household; number of males; number of females; total number in household. The returns are very incomplete. This census is in manuscript form only and is not available through interlibrary loan. This is not available at the FHL.

1857: Name; age; sex; color; birthplace; voting status of male (native or naturalized); occupation of each male over the age of 15. Microfilm index by last name. This was a territorial census taken by the Federal Government.

1865: Name; sex; color; deaf, dumb, blind, insane; soldier in service on June 1, 1865. This census is not complete for all counties. There are no schedules for the following counties that were formed before 1865: Aitkin, Anoka, Becker, Benton, Big Stone, Chippewa, Cottonwood, Douglas, Itasca, Kandiyohi, Kittson, Murray, Nobles, Otter Tail, Pipestone, Polk, Pope, Redwood, Renville, Rock, Stevens, Traverse, Wadena, Wilkin.

1875: Name; age; sex; color; birthplace (state or country); birthplaces of father and mother.

1885: Same information categories as 1875 but instead of parents' birthplaces, notes if father and mother of foreign birth; plus deaf, dumb, blind, insane; soldier in Civil War.

1895: Same information categories as 1885 plus length of residence in the state and the particular enumeration district (years and months) of males over age 21; occupation; months regularly employed in previous year; if previously enumerated in census; omits deaf, dumb, blind, insane.

1905: Same information categories as 1895 plus street address; birthplaces of father and mother (state or country); length of residence in the state and in the particular enumeration district for every person; service in Civil and Spanish-American wars.

There are printed inventories for the Minnesota state censuses of 1865, 1875, 1885, 1895, and 1905. These describe what counties are included for that year, lists the reel of microfilm on which a specific county may be found, and lists the order of the towns, townships, cities, etc. for each county. There is also a partial card index (incomplete even for the counties it does include) at the Minnesota Historical Society for the 1895 census covering only the counties of Aitkin, Anoka, Becker, Beltrami, and Big Stone.

The 1857, 1865, 1875, 1885, 1895, and 1905 state censuses are available on microfilm through interlibrary loan. Further information can be obtained by writing to Interlibrary Loan c/o Minnesota Historical Society.

The microfilms of the state censuses and copies of the printed inventories may also be purchased. For more information write to the Order Department at the Society.

Many thanks to Paula Stuart Warren, C.G.R.S., and Kathryn Ericson for their help with this section.

MISSISSIPPI

Territorial and state censuses are located at:

Mississippi Department of Archives and History
Archives and Library Division
P.O. Box 571
Jackson, Mississippi 39205

Some early censuses were taken by the Spanish in the colonial period; see the list at the end of this section for more information. Territorial and state censuses were taken several times from 1792 to 1866. They name only the head of household. In some cases the household in which a birth or death occurred in that year is indicated, but the name of the person who was born or who died is not given. Some of the censuses give the totals of males, females, and sometimes voters. Census records from 1818 to 1829 have been indexed in Donna Pannell, *Early State Census & Vital Statistics Records* (Mississippi Department of Archives and History, 1986). Indexing of the later years is in progress.

The following is a list of state and territorial censuses by county on microfilm at the Department of Archives and History. Those censuses that indicate births and deaths or have totals are so noted:

Adams: 1816, 1818, 1823 (births and deaths), 1830 (Natchez only), 1841, 1853 (excluding Natchez)
Amite: 1810, 1816, 1820, 1824 (totals), 1830 (totals), 1833 (totals), 1845, 1853
Attala: 1841
Bainbridge (now Covington): 1823
Baldwin (a territorial county): 1810, 1816
Bolivar: 1841, 1866
Chickasaw: 1837, 1841
Choctaw: 1837, 1840 (totals), 1860, and one undated census
Claiborne: 1810, 1816, 1822 (births and deaths), 1823 (births and deaths), 1825 (totals), 1866
Clarke (a territorial county): 1816
Clarke: 1841 (totals), 1853
Coahoma: 1841
Copiah: 1822 (totals), 1824 (births and deaths), 1825 (totals), 1841, 1853
Covington: 1823 (totals), 1841
DeSoto: 1841 (totals)
Franklin: 1816, 1820, 1833 (totals), 1841

Greene: 1816, 1825 (totals), 1841 (totals), 1853
Hancock: 1823 (totals), 1825 (totals), 1830 (totals), 1840 (totals), 1853
Hinds: 1824 (births and deaths and totals), 1825 (totals), 1841 (totals), 1850
Holmes: 1866
Issaquena: 1866
Itawamba: 1837, 1841, 1853, 1860
Jackson: 1825, 1841 (totals)
Jasper: 1866
Jefferson: 1805, 1808, 1810, 1816, 1823 (births and deaths), 1825 (totals),
    1841 (totals), 1853, 1866
Jones: 1837, 1841, 1853
Kemper: 1837, 1841 (totals)
Lauderdale: 1841 (totals), 1853
Lawrence: 1823, 1824 (births and deaths), 1825 (totals), 1830 (totals), 1841
Leake: 1841
Lowndes: 1837
Madison: 1841
Marion: 1816, 1820, 1823 (totals), 1825 (totals), 1841, 1866
Marshall: 1841
Monroe (a territorial county): 1816
Monroe: 1841
Neshoba: 1841, 1845
Newton: 1845
Noxubee: 1841 (totals), 1845, 1853
Oktibbeha: 1837, 1841, 1845
Panola: 1837, 1841, 1845, 1853
Perry: 1823 (births and deaths), 1825 (totals), 1841 (totals), 1845, 1853
Pike: 1816, 1820, 1825 (totals), 1830, 1841 (totals), 1845 (totals)
Pontotoc: 1837, 1845
Rankin: 1845, 1853
Scott: 1841, 1845
Simpson: 1824 (births and deaths), 1825 (totals), 1837, 1841, 1845 (totals),
    1866
Smith: 1841, 1845, 1866
Sunflower: 1845
Tallahatchie: 1841, 1845 (totals)
Tippah: 1841, 1845 (totals)
Tishomingo: 1837, 1841 (totals), 1845
Tunica: 1841, 1845 (totals)
Warren: 1810, 1816, 1825 (totals), 1845
Washington (a territorial county): 1808, 1810
Washington: 1841, 1845 (totals)
Wayne: 1816, 1820, 1841, 1845, 1853, 1866

Wilkinson: 1805, 1813, 1816, 1820, 1822 (births and deaths), 1823 (births
    and deaths), 1825, 1845
Winston: 1837, 1845 (totals), 1853
Yalobusha: 1845
Yazoo: 1824 (totals), 1825 (totals), 1841, 1845 (totals)

The FHL catalog also lists these additional censuses:

Covington: 1825
Franklin: 1810
Jefferson: 1822
Lawrence: 1818
Leake: 1853
Marion: 1824
Perry: 1822

Many of these censuses have been published:

> Roscoe R. Hill, *Descriptive Catalogue of the Documents Relating to the History of
> the United States in the Papeles Procedentes de Cuba Deposited in the Archivo
> General de Indias* (1916, repr. New York, 1965); provides information on
> the Spanish colonial period censuses of 1784, 1787, 1788, and 1784.

> "Adams County, Mississippi, Census, 1816," *National Genealogical Society
> Quarterly*, 37(1949):95.

> Mrs. Jerome A. Esker, "Census of 1816, Amite County, Mississippi Terri-
> tory," *National Genealogical Society Quarterly*, 53(1945):104.

> Ben Strickland and Jean Strickland, *Records of Greene County, Mississippi*
> (Milton, FL, 1980); includes the 1816 census.

> Ben Strickland and Jean Strickland, *Records of Jones County, Mississippi:
> 1827-1841 Tax Rolls, 1837, 1841, 1853 State Census* (Moss Point, MS,
> 1983).

> "Jones County, Mississippi - 1837 State Census Record," *Mississippi Genea-
> logical Exchange*, 16(1970):39.

> "Kemper County, Mississippi - 1837 State Census Record," *Mississippi Gene-
> alogical Exchange*, 18(1972):31.

> E. Russ Williams, *Records of Marion County, Mississippi*, Vol. 3 (Bogalusa, LA,
> 1965); includes the 1816 census.

> Winston DeVille, "Natchez 1723 Census," *National Genealogical Society
> Quarterly*, 59(1971):94.

Norman E. Gillis, *Early Inhabitants of the Natchez District* (Baton Rouge, 1963); includes the heads of households in 1792, 1810, and 1816 for the modern counties of Adams, Amite, Claiborne, Franklin, Jefferson, Warren, and Wilkinson.

"Newton County, Mississippi - 1845 State Census," *Mississippi Genealogical Exchange*, 26(1980):2.

"Panola County, Mississippi - 1837 State Census Record," *Mississippi Genealogical Exchange*, 19(1973):11.

Ben Strickland and Jean Strickland, *1841-1847 Tax Rolls; 1845 & 1853 State Census*, Vol. 4, *Records of Perry County, Mississippi* (Moss Point, MS, 1982).

"Pontotoc County, Mississippi - 1837 State Census," *Mississippi Genealogical Exchange*, 25(1979):29.

"Sunflower County, Mississippi - 1845 State Census," *Mississippi Genealogical Exchange*, 24(1978):81.

"Tishomingo County, Mississippi - 1837 State Census," *Mississippi Genealogical Exchange*, 17(1971):11.

"1841 State Census - Tunico Co., Mississippi," *Mississippi Genealogical Exchange*, 16(1970):11.

Ben Strickland and Jean Strickland, *State Census 1816, 1820, 1841, 1845, 1853, 1866*, Vol. 1, *Records of Wayne County, Mississippi* (Moss Point, MS, 1981).

Many thanks to Ruth Land Hatten, C.G.R.S., for her help with this section.

MISSOURI

Missouri took several state censuses, but very few copies survive. What does exist will be found in the county courthouses in the office of the Clerk of the County Court and on microfilm at:

Missouri State Archives
P.O. Box 778
600 West Main
Jefferson City, Missouri, 65102

Censuses were taken during the territorial period in 1814, 1817, and 1819, but only statistical summaries remain. There are listings of heads of families of New Madrid district for 1797 and 1803. Heads of families were enumerated for St. Charles district in 1817 and 1819 only (New Madrid and St. Charles were original districts and would cover a larger geographical area than the current counties of these names). Some of the early Spanish censuses of Upper Louisiana have been retrieved from the archives in Seville, Spain, and were published in Louis Houck's *The Spanish Regime in Missouri*, 2 vols. (Chicago, 1909), and in Lawrence Feldman's *Anglo-Americans in Spanish Archives* (Baltimore, 1991).

Although Missouri conducted a number of state censuses, most of the individual schedules are lost; only the statistical abstracts remain. The state did compile a census corresponding to the 1840 federal census. Nine of those enumerations survived the capitol building fire of 1911. They are for the counties of New Madrid, Newton, Pike, Randolph, Ray, Shelby, Stoddard, Warren, and Rives* (now Henry and St. Clair). The originals are located in the Missouri State Archives. A few listings remain for the state censuses of 1844 (Callaway and Greene counties), 1852, 1856, and 1868 (Cape Girardeau County); most of these are statistical abstracts only. The state census of 1876 exists for Benton, Butler, Callaway, Cape Girardeau*, Christian*, Franklin, Greene, Holt*, Howard*, Iron, McDonald*, Montgomery, Osage*, Phelps, Reynolds*, St. Francois, and Texas counties. The originals of these censuses remain in the county at the office of the Clerk of the County Court, but microfilmed copies have been made by the Missouri State Archives and can be searched there; the FHL does not have the counties of Franklin, Greene, Montgomery, and Osage. The above censuses with an asterisk (*) are either published, indexed, or both. In addition, the Greene County 1876 census has been indexed by the Greene County Archives and Records Center and is available from them.

Schuyler County took a special census in 1880. This and the above censuses are not enumerations of entire households, merely heads of households with others in the household enumerated by age groups similar to the federal population schedules before 1850. They include the number of deaf, dumb, blind, insane, the number of livestock, and some agricultural items.

The microfilms of the above censuses are for sale for $5.00 per reel from the State Archives, which will also do a limited amount of searching by mail. For such a search, first request "Genealogical Request Form AR-5P2" from the Archives.

Some of these censuses have been published:

Jacqueline Hogan Williams and Betty Harvey Williams, *1876 Benton County, Missouri State Census* (Warrensburg, 1969).

Thelma S. McManus and Robert E. Parkin, *1876 State Census, Butler County, Missouri* (St. Louis, 1981).

Quinton Keller and Jo Ann Keller, *Census of Cape Girardeau County, Missouri Taken in [1876]* (St. Louis, 1974).

Robert E. Parkin, *1864 State Census, Gasconade County, Missouri* (St. Louis, 1980).

Millie Preissle and Edward Preissle, *1876 Census of the County of Iron, State of Missouri* (Houston, 1983).

Melvin B. Goe, *Enumeration of the County of St. Charles, Missouri Territory, for the Years 1817 and 1819* (Utica, 1980).

Millie Preissle and Edward Preissle, *1876 Census, County of Texas, State of Missouri* (Houston, 1983).

Many thanks to Marsha Hoffman Rising for her help with this section.

MONTANA

Montana does not have any state censuses but it does have two items that can be used to locate people in the state. The Montana Historical Society in 1876 published "List of Early Settlers: A List of All Persons (Except Indians) Who Were in What is Now Montana During the Winter of 1862-63, Which Was the First Winter After the Gold Mines of This Region Had Become Noised Abroad," in *Contributions to the Historical Society of Montana*, volume 1. Names are arranged alphabetically by geographic area and the areas included are: "At Bannack City and vicinity (Dakotah Territory)," "Females at Bannack," "At Big Hole Bridge (Dakotah Territory)," "In Deer Lodge Valley (Washington Territory)," "List of citizens living at Ft. Benton," and "A list of white persons who resided in Missoula county (Washington Territory)."

The Territorial Secretary produced a poll list of registered voters for the October 1864 election (not available at the FHL). This list does not contain personal information about the voters. This is available at:

Montana Historical Society Library
225 N. Roberts Street
Helena, Montana 59620

NEBRASKA

The territorial censuses and 1885 state census are available at:

Nebraska State Historical Society
1500 R Street
Lincoln, Nebraska 68508

Sylvia Nimmo's article "Nebraska Research" (*National Genealogical Society Quarterly*, 77(1989):260) has the following information on state and territorial censuses. Territorial censuses were taken in eastern Nebraska in 1854, 1855, 1856, 1865, and 1869 naming the heads of household only. They still exist for a few counties, are available at the State Historical Society, and were published in the following volumes of *Nebraska and Midwest Genealogical Records*:

1854: Territory of Nebraska (volume 13).

1855: Nemaha, Otoe, Pawnee, and Richardson counties (volume 14); Cass, Dodge, Douglas, and Washington counties (volume 15).

1856: Nemaha, Otoe, Pawnee, and Richardson counties (volume 16); Cass, Clay, Cuming, Dodge, Douglas, Lancaster, and Platte counties (volume 17); Burt, Douglas (northern district), and Washington counties (volume 18); Dakota County (volume 19).

1865: Otoe County (volumes 19, 20, 21); Cuming County (volume 22).

1869: Butler and Stanton counties (volume 22).

The Deborah Avery Chapter of the Daughters of the American Revolution has published the *Census Records of Lancaster County, Nebraska, 1856-1874* (Lincoln, Nebraska, 1940). This includes the censuses for the years 1856, 1865, 1867, 1870, and 1874.

Ronald Vern Jackson has published *1854 1855 1856 Nebraska Territorial Census Index* (AIS, 1980).

The 1885 state census was co-sponsored by the federal government. The content is similar to the 1880 census and includes mortality, agricultural, and industrial schedules as well as the population schedule. A partial card index to the counties of Burt, Butler, Colfax, Cuming, Dodge, rural Douglas, Saline, Sarpy, Saunders, Stanton, and Washington has been prepared by the Eastern Nebraska Genealogical Society.

The State Historical Society has a microfilmed, alphabetical card file to the 1886 *Nebraska State Gazetteer and Business Directory*, which facilitates use of the 1885 census by identifying a county of residence. Information on the cards includes name, occupation, post office, county, and directory page number.

The State Historical Society also has some school censuses beginning in 1860; other school censuses may be found in the office of the county or city superintendent of schools. In addition to the names of children aged five to twenty-one, they include for each child the names of parents or guardians; birthplaces of parents; whether parents are living or dead; identity of guardian and relationship to child; address, race, birth date and place of child; and school attended or place of employment. Some may also include the place to or from which students transferred. The more recent of these records will be confidential.

NEVADA

The territorial census of 1862-3 and the state census of 1875 are available at:

Nevada State Library and Archives
Division of Archives and Records
101 S. Fall Street
Carson City, Nevada 89710

The 1872 state census is available at the Office of the Secretary of State, Carson City, Nevada.

The territorial census is only partially complete. The 1875 census names all members of the household and is indexed at the State Library. An index is also available at the library of the National Society of the Daughters of the American Revolution in Washington, D.C.

NEW JERSEY

Original and microfilm copies of the state censuses for 1855, 1865, 1875, 1885, 1895, 1905 and 1915 are available at:

Division of Archives and Records Management
Archives Section
Department of State
CN 307
185 W. State Street
Trenton, New Jersey 08625

Researchers may want to consult Bette Marie Barker, Daniel P. Jones, and Karl J. Niederer's *Guide to Family History Sources in the New Jersey State Archives*, 2nd. ed. (Trenton, 1990).

New Jersey took the following state censuses:

1855: Contains name (usually only head of household); number of adults in each household, subdivided by nativity (native-born or foreign-born), race (colored or white), and sex; and number of children aged 5 to 16 in each household, subdivided by race and gender. A few townships list all household members by name. Incomplete records exist for the counties of Atlantic, Bergen, Camden, Cumberland, Essex (including present-day Union county), Gloucester, Hunterdon, Hudson, Monmouth, Morris, Passaic, Somerset, Sussex, and Warren.

1865: Contains name (all members of the household), sex, whether native or foreign-born, whether colored or white, and whether school-aged (5 to 16 years). Incomplete records exist for the counties of Atlantic, Bergen, Burlington, Camden, Cumberland, Essex, Gloucester, Hudson, Hunterdon, Middlesex, Monmonth, Passaic, Salem, Sussex, and Union.

1875: Contains name (all members of the household), age, sex, native- or foreign-born, color, birthplace of individual and parents, and occupation. Incomplete records exist only for the two counties of Essex and Sussex.

1885: Complete for the state and contains name, sex, race, age in categories of under 5, 5-20, 20-60, and over 60, and native- or foreign-born (Irish, German, and other).

1895: Complete for the state and contains name, sex, race, age in categories of under 5, 5-20, 20-60, and over 60, and native- or foreign-born (Irish, German, and other).

1905: Complete for the state and contains name, color, sex, month and year of birth, marital status, birthplace, parents' birthplaces, number of years in U.S., citizenship status, occupation, whether literate or fluent in English, and whether home is owned or rented. In urban areas street names and house numbers are provided.

1915: Complete for the state and contains name, color, sex, month and year of birth, age, marital status, birthplace, parents' birthplaces, number of years in U.S., citizenship status, occupation, whether literate or fluent in English, and whether home is owned or rented. In urban areas street names and house numbers are provided.

Many thanks to Roger Joslyn, C.G., F.A.S.G, for his help with this section.

NEW MEXICO

The Spanish and Mexican censuses for the Province of New Mexico and the 1885 territorial census are available at:

> State of New Mexico
> State Records Center and Archives
> 404 Montezuma
> Santa Fe, New Mexico 87503

The early Spanish and Mexican censuses for the New Mexico area have been published in three books: Virginia Langham Olmsted, *Spanish and Mexican Colonial Censuses of New Mexico: 1790, 1823, 1845* (Albuquerque, 1976); Donald S. Dreesen, *Late Spanish Censuses of the Rio Abajo, New Mexico* (author, 1980); and Virginia Langham Olmsted, *Spanish and Mexican Censuses of New Mexico: 1750-1830* (Albuquerque, 1981). In the Introduction to her first volume, Virginia Olmsted says that "although each census is fragmentary with many communities missing, the combined censuses constitute a primary source for locating original homes of the colonial families of New Mexico." The information to be found in the early census records is as follows:

> The 1790 Spanish census is much more informative than the 1790 census of the United States. In addition to the names of the heads of household, the following facts are given: age, ethnic derivation, occupation, marital status, wife's name and age, plus the number, age and sex of children, other relatives and servants within the household.

> The 1823 Mexican census has a wealth of family information but is, unfortunately, the most fragmentary of the three enumerations. Every member of the household is listed by name, age, marital status and occupation.

> The 1845 Mexican census contains the most complete community listing of any enumeration, but the content for each one varies with the individual enumerator, and there is no consistent pattern of information.

The 1885 territorial census names all members of the household; relationship to head of household; sex; race; age; marital status; born within the year; married within the year; profession, occupation, or trade; number of months unemployed during census year; whether person is sick or temporarily disabled; whether blind, deaf, or insane; attended school within the year; ability to read and write; and place of birth of person, father, and mother. This was a federal census so copies are also available at the National Archives.

Like the 1880 federal census, the 1885 territorial census has additional mortality, agricultural, and industrial schedules. There is also a listing of Union and Confederate veterans of the Civil War and an enumeration of land grants by county. Ralph L. Hayes published a "Users Guide to the 1885 Territorial Census" in the *New Mexico Genealogist*, 25(1986). This is a detailed listing of the reel and page numbers on which the information from the population, mortality, agricultural, or industrial schedules can be found for each town or precinct within each county. This is particularly useful because there are unfortunate gaps in this census. For example, the population schedules are missing for the counties of Bernalillo (one page is extant), Rio Arriba, and Santa Fe, and the census for Grant County is virtually illegible.

Several articles have been published on New Mexico censuses for specific towns, counties, or areas:

> Donald S. Dreesen and Robert W. Delaney, "Census of the Pueblo of San Juan de los Caballeros of the Tegua Nation - and of the Pueblo of San Lorenzo de los Picuris - and of the Parish of Santa Cruz de los Espanoles - of the Year of 1707," *New Mexico Genealogist*, 28(1989).

> "Spaniards from the Jurisdiction of Taos, 1790," *New Mexico Genealogist*, 21(1982); contains additional information on Taos for the 1790 census.

> Julian Josue Vigil, "Galisteo, Sante Fe County, NM Census, circa 1830," *New Mexico Genealogist*, 26(1987).

> "1893 Special Census for Precinct 7" of Sante Fe County was published in the *New Mexico Genealogist* 22(1983) and the original enumeration book is at the Records Center and Archives. Precinct 7 (Cerrillos) was part of the first district lying south of the Santa Fe River. This census gives only name and age. Before publication, this census was compared with the 1900 federal census for Cerrillos and those persons also appearing in 1900 have been marked and variations in spellings of surnames have been indicated.

> John Walker Buchner, "1904 Census Weed, Pinon, Avis, and McDonald Flats," *Peco Trails*, 3(1983).

Ralph L. Hayes, "Census of Columbus, Luna Co., N.M. in 1913," *New Mexico Genealogist*, 26(1987):41. The original of this census is also at the Records Center and Archives. It includes the name, occupation, age, and sex of the residents.

The State Records Center and Archives also has the following censuses:

Census of Las Huertas and Bernalillo, 1802
Census of Jemez, 1845
Census of Taos, 1847
Census of Tecolote, 1855 (Pct. 4)
Census of the city of Sante Fe, 1891
Census of Belen, 1918
Census of Los Lunas, 1928

Many thanks to Ralph L. Hayes and Betty Likes Clarke for their help with this section.

NEW YORK

The New York state censuses are not available in any one location, though the New York State Library in Albany does have microfilm copies for the entire state for 1915 and 1925 and many of the earlier state censuses. Most of the originals are still to be found in the offices of the county clerks, though some are with the county historian. Some counties will search the censuses in response to a mail request, though there may be a fee.

Many have been microfilmed, so copies may be available through the Family History Library, the New York State Library in Albany, or The New York Public Library and the New York Genealogical and Biographical Society in New York City. A list of the state censuses on microfilm at the State Library is available from them, and a list of the holdings of the 1855, 1865, and 1875 state censuses appeared in the Spring 1990 issue of *The NYG&B Newsletter*. This issue of the *Newsletter* also noted that The New York Public Library had acquired the 1915 and 1925 state censuses for the five New York City counties plus Nassau, Suffolk, and Westchester.

A few census records have been published such as Albany County for 1790 and the 1825 census for Cortland, Lewis, and Yates counties by the Central New York Genealogical Society. There are also some published indexes such as those by David Davenport for Montgomery, Schenectady, and Schoharie counties for 1855, and by Fred Bowman for 1855 Greene County. Other indexes exist in manuscript form and some of these have been microfilmed; these include Allegany (1855), Broome (1855), Cayuga (1855), Cortland (1855), Delaware (1855), Erie (1855), Herkimer (1855, 1865, 1875), Madison (1855), Monroe (1855), Niagara (1855, 1865, 1875), and Wayne (1855, 1865, 1875).

New York Area Key, A Guide to the Genealogical Records of the State of New York Including Maps, Histories, Charts, and Other Helpful Materials, by Florence Clint, has helpful forms that can be used for abstracting the information from the New York state censuses. Also useful is David Paul Davenport's article "The State Censuses of New York, 1825-1875," *Genealogical Journal*, 14(1985-6):172.

For a listing of the available New York state censuses for each county and where they are located, see Marilyn Douglas and Melinda Yates, *New York State Census Records, 1790-1925* (Bibliography Bulletin 88, The University of the State of New York, 1981). This publication does have a few errors of omission. To order send $3.00 (make check payable to the New York State Library) to:

> Gifts and Exchange
> New York State Library
> Cultural Education Center
> Albany, New York 12230

New York took the following state censuses:

1790: Only Albany County is known to survive and was published by Kenneth Scott in *New York: State Census of Albany County Towns in 1790* (1975; repr. Baltimore, 1991).

1825: Names the head of household; number of males; number of females; males in family subject to militia duty (ages 18-45); male voters; aliens not naturalized; paupers, untaxed colored persons; taxable colored persons; colored voters; married females under 45 years of age; unmarried females ages 16-45; marriages in the previous year; births in the previous year (male and female); deaths in the previous year (male and female).

1835: Same as 1825.

1845: Has the same information as the 1825 and 1835 censuses with these additional columns: born in New York; born in New England; born in other states; born in Latin America; born in British Empire; born in France; born in Germany; born in other nations of Europe; children age 5-16; school children.

The 1845 state census of Indians includes nine Iroquois tribes living on eight reservations. It names the head of household (names are often given in the original tongue together with a translation) and then gives family statistics. Questions about land include the number of acres of meadow cut, lands rented out to white men, land cultivated by others, value of proceeds from the "chace" (hunting ground), and the value of gardens exclusive of family consumption. Other statistics include the number of farmers, mechanics, physicians, teachers, catechists, lawyers, interpreters and translators of the Iroquois, church members of all denominations, the number who retained their native religion, and the number of those enrolled or pledged to temperance.

1855: Names all members of the household; age; sex; color or race; relation to family head; county of New York, state, or country of birth; now married; now widowed; years resident in this city or town; profession, trade, or occupation; native voters; naturalized voters; aliens; colored persons not taxed; land owner; over 21 and illiterate; deaf, dumb, blind, insane, or idiotic.

This census also includes enumerations of those who were married or died within the previous year. Unfortunately, they are practically useless, since the names of the married couple or the deceased were not given. For further information see David Davenport, "The State Censuses of New York, 1825-1875," *Genealogical Journal*, 14(1985-6):187.

1865: Names all members of the household (including those absent in army or navy); age; sex; color; relation to family head; county of New York, state, or country of birth; parent of how many children; number of times married; marital status; profession, trade, or occupation; usual place of employment; native and naturalized voters; aliens; colored persons not taxed; owners of land; over 21 and illiterate; deaf, dumb, blind, insane, or idiotic; servicemen (lists those now or formerly in the army or navy of the U.S.).

This census also includes enumerations for those who were married or died within the previous year. The marriage enumeration includes the names of the groom and bride, their ages, previous civil condition, the month and day of the ceremony, the city or town in which the marriage took place, and whether the marriage was solemnized by a clergyman, by a civil magistrate, or by declaration before witnesses. The death schedules include the name of the deceased, their age, sex, color, civil condition, month and day of death, state or country of birth (often the county of birth for those born in New York), occupation, and cause of death. For further information see the article by Davenport referred to above.

Two towns in the 1865 state census have been found to have the special feature of including the maiden names of wives. These are Horseheads in Chemung County, and one election district of Watervliet in Albany County.

1875: Names all members of the household; age; sex; color; relation to family head; county of New York, state, or country of birth; marital status; profession, trade, or occupation; usual place of employment (those in military service list former home); native employment (those in military service list former home); native and naturalized voters; aliens; owners of land; over 21 and illiterate; deaf, dumb, blind, insane, or idiotic.

This census also includes enumerations of those who were married or died within the previous year. The information is the same as in 1865.

1892: Names all members of the household; sex; age; color; country of birth; citizen or alien; occupation, trade, profession, or kind of work done by each person. This census does not have dwelling house or family numbers, so it is sometimes difficult to tell where one family ends and another begins.

1905: Names all members of the household; relation to family head; color; sex; age; country of birth; number of years in the U.S.; citizen or alien; occupation, trade, profession, or kind of work done by each person; previous residence of Institutional Inmates before being admitted.

1915: Names all members of the household; color; sex; age; country of birth; number of years in the U.S.; citizen or alien; if naturalized, when and where (1925); occupation; previous residence of Institutional Inmates before being admitted; infants under one year.

1925: Same as 1915.

Many thanks to Roger Joslyn, C.G., F.A.S.G., for his help with this section.

NORTH CAROLINA

Alvaretta Kenan Register has published the *State Census of North Carolina 1784-1787*, 2nd ed. (Baltimore, 1973). This census contains the name of the head of household and then the number of white males from 21 to 60, white males under 21 and above 60, white females of every age, blacks of each sex from 12 to 50, and blacks upwards of 50 and under 12. There are some counties for which only summaries without names survive. The following counties survive with names:

Bertie	Hyde	Pasquotank
Burke	Johnston	Perquimans
Caswell	Jones	Pitt
Chowan	Martin	Richmond
Duplin	Montgomery	Surry
Gates	New Hanover	Tyrrell
Granville	Northampton	Warren
Halifax	Onslow	Wilkes

Corrections and additions were published in *North Carolina Genealogy*:

"1786 Census of North Carolina," 13(1967):1996.

"Granville Co.: 1786 Census," 14(1968):2155.

"1784-7 Census of North Carolina (Additions and Corrections)," 21(1975):3128.

And in *The North Carolina Genealogical Society Journal*:

Jonathan B. Butcher, "1787 Census Return for Pearson's Company, Rowan County, N.C.," 11(1985):253.

NORTH DAKOTA

The 1885 census for the northern half of the Datoka Territory and the 1915 and 1925 state censuses are available at:

> State Archives and Historical Research Library
> State Historical Society of North Dakota
> North Dakota Heritage Center
> 612 East Boulevard Avenue
> Bismarck, North Dakota 58505-0830

1885: Names all members of the household. Also includes schedules of agriculture, manufacture, Civil War veterans, and mortality.

1915: Names all members of the household. It is not indexed.

1925: Same as 1915.

The State Historical Society also has the 1857 census for Pembina County which was then a part of the Minnesota Territory.

The State Historical Society will search all the above censuses, as well as the federal censuses, for $1.00 per household, for each census, and for each county searched. But since the state censuses are not indexed, precise locations must be provided for the search. Forms entitled "Request for Census Record Search" are available from the above address. These censuses are also available through Interlibrary Loan.

Many thanks to Adrienne Stepanek, C.G.R.S., for her help with this section.

OHIO

Ohio did not take any state censuses, but starting in 1803 a census of eligible voters (Quadrennial Enumerations) was taken every four years as required by the first Ohio Constitution. At that time the only eligible voters in Ohio were free white males age 21 or older. Quadrennial enumerations were taken by township and are organized either alphabetically or in order of visitation. They list the head of household and either the number or names of other eligible voters in the household. There was also an earlier 1800 territorial census which preceded statehood and listed the names of eligible voters under the names of the heads of the households in which they lived.

As time went on the criteria for these quadrennial enumerations changed to fit the interests of the state government in tabulating its inhabitants. From 1863 on, black males were included and by 1883 the post office addresses and occupations were added along with an indication as to whether the resident was a freeholder or not. Michael L. Hausman has published "Belmont County, Ohio, Census of Blacks, 1863," in the *National Genealogical Society Quarterly*, 69(1981).

Unfortunately, few of Ohio's quadrennial enumerations have been found. The misconception that all enumerations taken from 1803 to 1911 are in existence has led many to search in vain. The records that do still exist are not housed in one archive. Most are distributed among the Ohio "Network of American History Research Centers" created in 1970. These centers, with their coded abbreviations, are as follows:

Archives Services, Bierce Library (UA)
University of Akron
Akron, OH 44325-1750

Center for Archival Collections (BG)
Bowling Green State University
Bowling Green, OH 43403-0175

Archives and Rare Books Department (UC)
Blegen Library
University of Cincinnati
Cincinnati, OH 45221-0113

Archives-Library Division (OHS)

Ohio Historical Society
1982 Velma Avenue
Columbus, OH 43211-1497

Archives and Special Collections (OU)
Alden Library, Ohio University
Athens, OH 45701-2978

Western Reserve Historical Society (WR)
10825 East Boulevard
Cleveland, OH 44106-1788

Archives and Special Collections (WSU)
Wright State University Library
Dayton, OH 45435-0001

Ohio took the following territorial and quadrennial enumerations:

1800: The original Washington county territorial enumeration is at the Campus Martius Museum, Marietta, Ohio, but a typed copy titled "Census of Washington County, Ohio - 1800" is available at Ohio University. Both the head of household and other eligible voters within the household are named. These other eligible voters are indented under the heads of their respective households. At that time Washington County encompassed a large area extending into the present counties of Holmes, Tuscarawas, Coshocton, Guernsey, Muskingum, Noble, Morgan, Perry, Athens, Vinton, Hocking, and Meigs.

1801: The Family History Library has an 1801 Clermont County census that was microfilmed at the Western Reserve Historical Society.

1803: The 1803 enumeration was for Washington, but as stated above, this county then covered a much larger area. Some enumerators recorded this census alphabetically (OU).

1807: The 1807 enumeration was published in 1968 and can be purchased from The Butler County Genealogical Society, P.O. Box 2011, Middletown, OH 45044. The Family History Library has a typescript of the 1807 enumeration for Highland County bound with the *Index to A History of the Early Settlement of Highland County*.

1811: Enumerations exist for Ashtabula County (WR).

1819: Enumerations exist for Loramie and Turtle Creek townships in Shelby County (WSU) and Clermont County (Family History Library). The FHL catalog also lists Ashtabula County.

1823: Enumerations exist for Amanda, Cynthian, Green, Loramie, Orange, Perry, and Turtle Creek townships in Shelby County (WSU). The FHL catalog also lists Ashtabula County.

1827: Enumerations exist for Allen, Miami, and Shelby counties (WSU). The FHL catalog also lists Ashtabula County.

1831: Enumerations exist for Fairfield and Portage counties (OHS), and Shelby County (WSU).

1835: Enumerations exist for Ashtabula County (WR), and Miami and Shelby counties (WSU). The FHL catalog also lists Portage County.

1837: This was not a quadrennial year and may be a mistake for 1827. Enumerations exist for St. Mary's and Dublin townships in Mercer County and Willshire township in Van Wert County (WSU).

1839: Enumerations exist for Fairfield County (OHS). The FHL catalog also lists Portage County.

1843: Enumerations exist for Mercer and Shelby counties (WSU). The FHL catalog also lists Ashtabula County.

1847: Enumerations exist for German and St. Mary's townships in Auglaize County (then part of Mercer County), Logan County, Mercer County, and Shelby County (WSU), and for Perry County (OU, OHS).

The following list is for quadrennial enumerations after 1850 by county:

Allen: 1883, 1887 (BG)
Athens: 1887, 1903 (OU)
Auglaize: 1851, 1855, 1859, 1863, 1883, 1891, 1895, 1903, 1907 (also 1860 for Jackson township and 1861 for Clay township, though neither of these were enumeration years) (WSU)

Brown: 1887, 1891, 1903 (OHS, UC)

Clinton: 1907 (OHS, UC)

Columbiana: 1899, 1903 (OHS, FHL)

Coshocton: 1883, 1891 (OHS)

Darke: 1887 (WSU)

Delaware: 1887 (OHS)

Fairfield: 1851, 1859 (OHS)

Fayette: 1887, 1891, 1899 (OHS)

Gallia: 1899 (OU, FHL)

Hardin: 1887, 1891, 1895, 1899, 1903, 1907 (Family History Library micro-filmed original records at courthouse)

Jefferson: 1883-1907 (OHS)

Lawrence: 1891-1907 (OU)

Mercer: 1855; 1859 except Dublin township; 1875 for Butler, Center, Dublin, Gibson, and Hopewell townships; 1879; 1895; 1899; 1903 for Black Creek, Butler, Franklin, Gibson, Granville, and Recovery townships and 3 precincts in Dublin township; 1907 for Black Creek, Butler, Franklin, Granville, Hopewell, Jefferson, and Washington townships, wards 1-4 of Celina, 3 precincts of Marion township, 2 precincts of Recovery township, and the village of Rockford (WSU)

Morrow: 1867; 1871-1883; 1891-1907 (OHS)

Perry: 1847-1871; 1879-1887 (OU, OHS)

Pickaway: 1891-1903 (OHS)

Portage: 1831-1839 (OHS)

Preble: 1882 (WSU)

Seneca: 1899, 1903 (BG, FHL)

Shelby: 1851; 1855; 1859; 1863; 1871; 1875 for Cynthian, Dinsmore, Franklin, Loramie, McLean, Orange, Salem, Turtle Creek, Van Buren, and Washington townships (WSU)

Van Wert: 1887 (BG)

Washington: 1887, 1911 (OHS)

Wood: 1899 (BG)

Many thanks to Ann Fenley, Alma Aicholtz Smith, C.G.R.S., and W. Louis Phillips, C.G., for their help with this section.

OKLAHOMA

Oklahoma did not take any state censuses, but a special 1890 territorial census with a partial card index is available at:

Oklahoma State Historical Society
Wiley Post Historical Building
2100 N. Lincoln Boulevard
Oklahoma City, Oklahoma 73105

In June 1890, a special census was taken of persons residing in Oklahoma Territory's first seven counties. Six counties had been created from the Unassigned Lands in 1889. The seventh county, Beaver, was formed in 1890 and included all of the panhandle, which had variously been called No Man's Land, Public Land Strip, Cimarron Territory, and Robber's Roost. On the census the counties are designated only by number: 1st (Logan), 2nd (Oklahoma), 3rd (Cleveland), 4th (Canadian), 5th (Kingfisher), 6th (Payne), 7th (Beaver).

The original manuscripts are in the custody of the Oklahoma Historical Society and access is restricted. The original census sheets for Townships 14 North, Range 3 West and 14 North, Range 4 West (including the town of Edmond) are missing. The census has been microfilmed on one roll and can be purchased from the Society. The missing sheets and the following pages do not appear on the microfilm: page 273, a transmittal sheet; pages 652 and 654, a part of 9N-3W in Cleveland County; page 673, part of the city of Norman in Cleveland County.

Categories of information include name, relationship to head of household, color, sex, age, state or country of birth, number of years in the U.S., length of residence in the territory, data on naturalization, military service, and ability to read and write.

There is no complete index to the census. The Library Resources Division of the Oklahoma Historical Society has a card index compiled from the microfilm for the counties of Logan, Oklahoma, Cleveland, and Canadian. A published index for the remaining three is available: Vicki Sullivan and Mac R. Harris, *Index to the 1890 Oklahoma Territorial Census for the Counties of Kingfisher, Payne and Beaver* (Oklahoma City, 1977).

Researchers should note: The census enumerators were often unaware of the township boundaries or knowingly crossed them to save time later.

This resulted in some townships being listed in the wrong county and has caused discrepancies in both of the above indexes.

Two resources complement the 1890 census: James W. Smith, *Smith's First Directory of Oklahoma Territory for the Year Commencing August 1st 1890* (Guthrie, OK, n.d.), and the *Eleventh Census (1890) Enumerating Union Veterans and Widows of Union Veterans of the Civil War* (National Archives microfilm #76). The Oklahoma Genealogical Society has published an index to the entries on this roll.

Prior to the establishment of Oklahoma Territory in 1890, all of present-day Oklahoma, except the panhandle, was Indian Territory. The only federal census of the non-Indian residents before 1900 was taken in 1860. Census data for aliens (non-citizens) residing in the Indian Territory is sparse. Some Indian tribes attempted to enumerate this alien population - which grew from approximately 10,500 in 1860 to nearly 300,000 in 1900. The most complete census returns are for non-citizens residing in the Cherokee Nation. The 1880 and 1890 Cherokee National Censuses are two examples. These enumerations and others will be found in the Archives and Manuscript Division of the Oklahoma Historical Society, the National Archives, and the National Archives/Southwest Region in Fort Worth, Texas.

A special enumeration by the Bureau of the Census was taken in 1907. The only portion of this census known to be extant is for Seminole County which is in the custody of the National Archives.

The library staff at the Oklahoma Historical Society will answer requests for specific information. A "Biographical Research Request" form is available from the Library Resources Divison at the above address. Photocopies from microfilm are $1.00 per sheet and there is a $1.50 charge for postage and handling per request.

Many thanks to Sharron Standifer Ashton for her help with this section.

OREGON

Provisional, territorial, and state censuses for Oregon are available at:

Oregon State Archives
1005 Broadway NE.
Salem, Oregon 97310

Researchers may be interested in obtaining *Provisional, Territorial and State Census Records in the Oregon State Archives,* available from the State Archives.

Not all censuses still exist for each county or year. The following is a list of those censuses by county available at the State Archives:

1842: Persons living south of the Columbia River
1843: Elijah White Census
1845: Champoeg (now Marion), Clackamas, Clatsop, Tuality (now Washington), Yamhill
1845-46: Tuality (now Washington)
1849: Apportionment Census (males over 21): Benton, Champoeg (now Marion), Clackamas, Clatsop, Lewis (now in Washington State), Linn, Polk, Tuality (now Washington), Vancouver (now in Washington State), Yamhill
1850: Washington
1853: Marion, Polk, Umpqua (now Douglas), Washington, Benton
1854: Benton, Clatsop, Jackson
1855: Coos, Jackson
1856: Benton, Clackamas, Columbia, Curry, Polk, Washington
1857: Benton, Clackamas, Coos, Curry, Douglas, Jackson, Tillamook, Umpqua (now Douglas), Washington
1858: Benton, Clatsop, Coos, Curry, Umpqua (now Douglas)
1859: Clatsop, Umpqua (now Douglas)
1865: Benton, Columbia, Marion, Umatilla
1870: Umatilla
1875: Umatilla
1885: Linn, Umatilla
1895: Linn, Morrow, Multnomah, Marion
1905: Baker, Lane, Linn, Marion

Of the above censuses, the FHL does not have Polk County in 1853; Columbia County in 1856; Curry, Douglas, Tillamook, Umpqua, and

Washington counties in 1857; Benton, Clatsop, Curry, and Umpqua counties in 1858; nor any of the censuses after 1859. They do, however, list in their catalog an 1858 census for Jackson County.

RHODE ISLAND

Rhode Island has three early censuses that have been published:

John R. Bartlett, *Census of the Inhabitants of the Colony of Rhode Island and Providence Plantations 1774* (Baltimore, 1969). Contains the names of the heads of household, number of males and females under 16 and over 16, and the number of Indians and blacks in each household. New Shoreham was omitted, but is on microfilm at the Rhode Island State Archives.

Mildred M. Chamberlain, *Rhode Island 1777 Military Census* (Baltimore, 1985). This appeared first in *Rhode Island Roots* from December 1981 to September 1984. It names each man and says whether he is age 16 to 50 able or unable to bear arms, 50 to 60 able or unable to bear arms, 60 and upwards. It also lists those who have taken the affirmation, those who have certificates from the Friends Meetings, transient persons and to what places they belong, negroes, Indians, those in the State Militia, and those in Continental Service.

Jay Mack Holbrook, *Rhode Island 1782 Census* (Oxford, Mass. 1979). Contains the names of the heads of households and the males and females in the age categories of 0 to 15, 16 to 21, 22 to 49, and 50 and upwards. It also contains columns for the number of Indians, mulattoes, and blacks in each household. The originals for two towns, North Providence and Smithfield, were not found, so this book contains contemporary tax lists for these two towns.

Rhode Island took the following state censuses:

1865: Names all members of the household, age, sex, color, place of birth, parentage, cannot read or write (over 15), occupation (over 15), if naturalized voter, if attending school, if deaf and dumb, blind, insane or idiotic, employment in military or navy since 1860. For those born in Rhode Island it gives the town of birth. There is a full name index on cards for this census at the Rhode Island Historical Society and they will search for one individual for a fee of $15.00.

1875: Names all members of the household, age, sex, color, relationship to head of household, marital state, parentage, cannot read or write, occupation, voter, number of months in public, select or Catholic school.

1885: Names all members of the household, sex, relationship to head of family, color and race, age, marital state, place of birth, parentage, occupation, if cannot read or write (over 10), number of months in school, if blind, deaf and dumb, idiotic or insane, political condition of males 21 and over, if registered voter, real estate voter, personal property voter, naturalized or alien. There are separate alphabetical listings for males and females by towns, a copy of which is available on microfilm at the Rhode Island Historical Society.

1905: Names all members of the household, relationship to the head of family, color or race, age, conjugal condition, date of birth, number of children, place of birth, whether able to read and write, year of immigration, number of years in United States, number of years resident in Rhode Island, number of months resident during census year in town, birthplace of father and mother, occupation, number of months unemployed, whether a Union soldier, sailor or marine during Civil or Spanish-American War, pension, religion. There are separate alphabetical listings for males and females by towns. (At the time of this writing this census was being transferred to another format and was unavailable for research.) This is not available at the FHL.

1915: Names all members of the household, relationship to head of household, sex, color, age, place of birth, place of birth of father and mother, alien or naturalized, occupation, nature of business, employer, employee or working on own, if out of work. This census is organized by enumeration district and city directories will assist the researcher in determining the correct enumeration district. The 1915 census for Pawtucket is on microfilm at the Rhode Island Historical Society. This is not available at the FHL.

1925: Names all members of the household, relationship to head of household, sex, color, age, place of birth, citizenship. This census is organized by enumeration district and city directories will assist the researcher in determining the correct enumeration district. This is not available at the FHL.

1935: Names all members of the household, sex, race, place of birth, date of birth, marital status, if can read and write English, citizenship, if at school and name of school, grade in school, physical disabilities, occupation if unemployed- usually work, seeking work, usual occupation, why not at work, how long unemployed. This census is alphabetically arranged by town. This is not available at the FHL.

Microfilm copies of the 1865, 1875, and 1885 state censuses are available at:

The Rhode Island Historical Society Library
121 Hope Street
Providence, Rhode Island 02906

The originals of the 1865, 1875, 1885, 1905, 1915, 1925, and 1935 state censuses are available at:

Rhode Island State Archives
337 Westminster Street
Providence, Rhode Island 02903

Many thanks to Christine Lamar for her help with this section.

SOUTH CAROLINA

State censuses are available at:

South Carolina Department of Archives and History
1430 Senate Street
P.O. Box 11669
Columbia, South Carolina 29211

The Archives has population returns for Fairfield and Laurens districts in 1829 and for Kershaw and Chesterfield districts in 1839. The agricultural returns for 1868 and the population returns for 1869 are nearly complete. The schedules for Clarendon, Oconee, and Spartanburg counties are missing for 1869. The agricultural and population returns for 1875 are complete for the counties of Clarendon, Newberry, and Marlboro, and there are partial returns for the counties of Abbeville, Beaufort, Fairfield, Lancaster, and Sumter.

SOUTH DAKOTA

The 1885 federal and 1895, 1905, 1915, 1925, 1935, and 1945 state censuses are available at:

South Dakota State Historical Society
Cultural Heritage Center
900 Governors Drive
Pierre, South Dakota 57501-2217

The 1885 federal census for the Dakota Territory is available for the following counties: Beadle, Butte, Charles Mix, Edmunds, Fall River, Faulk, Hand, Hanson, Hutchinson, Hyde, Lake, Lincoln, Marshall, McPherson, Moody, Roberts, Sanborn, Spink, Stanley, Turner. This census names all members of the household.

The 1895 census is available for the counties of Beadle, Brule, Pratt (now Jones), Presho (now Lyman), Campbell, and Charles Mix. This census names all members of the household. Microfilms of both this and the 1885 census can be borrowed on Interlibrary Loan.

The censuses of 1905 through 1945 are available on file cards at the State Historical Society. They are arranged alphabetically by surname and then by first name. The Historical Society will search the state census records, but a pre-payment of $5.00 for each search is required. These censuses are not available at the FHL.

Many thanks to Adrienne Stepanek, C.G.R.S., for her help with this section.

TENNESSEE

An act of the General Assembly of Tennessee of 15 January 1891 provided for an enumeration of male inhabitants of twenty-one years of age and upward, citizens of Tennessee. The Tennessee State Library and Archives, 403 Seventh Avenue North, Nashville, Tennessee, 37219, has microfilmed this census. Sue S. Reed made a photocopy from the microfilm and then prepared indexes. Her typescripts are available at the FHL:

Volume 1: Anderson, Blount, Knox, and Sevier counties.
Volume 2: Benton, Carroll, Henry, Houston, and Stewart counties.
Volume 3: Dyer, Gibson, Lake, Obion, and Weakley counties.
Volume 4: Shelby County.
Volume 5: Cumberland, Fentress, Jackson, Loudon, Morgan, Overton, Putnam, Roane, and Scott counties.
Volume 6: Campbell, Clay, Hancock, Macon, Pickett, Smith, and Trousdale counties.

As is the case with almost all other states, the 1890 federal census for Tennessee was destroyed by fire, but the veterans census has been published by Byron Sistler, *1890 Civil War Veterans Census — Tennessee* (Evanston, Ill., 1978).

TEXAS

Texas did not take any censuses after statehood, but several mission or rancho censuses were taken under the Spanish and Mexican governments. These can be found in *Residents of Texas 1782-1836*, 3 vols. (San Antonio, 1984). The census taken under the Government of Mexico from 1829 to 1836 has also been published by Marion Day Mullins, *The First Census of Texas, 1829-1836, To Which are Added Texas Citizenship Lists, 1821-1845, and Other Early Records of the Republic of Texas* (reprinted as NGS Special Publication No. 22 from the *National Genealogical Society Quarterly*, 1959). It includes the names and ages of all members of the household and the occupations of the head of household. Also by Mullins, though not technically a census, is *Republic of Texas: Poll Lists for 1846* (Baltimore, 1974), which is an alphabetical list of about 18,000 heads of household, with county of residence.

UTAH

A territorial census was taken in Utah in 1856. An index to it has been published: Bryan Lee Dilts, *1856 Utah Census Index, An Every-Name Index* (Salt Lake City, 1983). As Mr. Dilts explains in his introduction, this census probably should be used with caution:

> Indeed, some names on the 1856 census seem to be fictitious, repeated, or those of non-residents of Utah Territory. For example, the names of several identical persons appear in different census districts. Some names listed on the 1856 Utah census are those of people who died while crossing the plains before 1856. Further, if a certain family had a daughter named Mary Louiza Roberts, that daughter might be listed under 1) Mary Roberts, 2) Louiza Roberts, and 3) Louiza Newel, her married name.

Another source that may help researchers locate people in Utah is the Index to the Bishops Report of 1852. This is an alphabetical list of the heads of household within each ward. It includes only members of The Church of Jesus Christ of Latter-day Saints and is available at the FHL.

VIRGINIA

The 1790 federal census for Virginia is missing, therefore several state censuses were used by the Census Bureau to prepare *Heads of Families, At the First Census of the United States Taken in the Year 1790, Records of the State Enumerations 1782 to 1785* (Washington, D.C., 1908). The following is a list of the counties with the years for which there is an enumeration from 1782 to 1785:

Albemarle, 1785
Amelia, 1782, 1785
Amherst, 1783, 1785
Charlotte, 1782
Chesterfield, 1783
Cumberland, 1782, 1784
Essex, 1783
Fairfax, 1782, 1785
F luvanna, 1782
Frederick, 1782
Gloucester, 1783, 1784
Greenbrier, 1783-1786
Greensville, 1783
Halifax, 1782, 1785
Hampshire, 1782, 1784
Hanover, 1782
Harrison, 1785
Isle of Wight, 1782
Lancaster, 1783, 1785
Mecklenburg, 1782
Middlesex, 1783
Monongalia, 1782
Nansemond, 1783, 1784
New Kent, 1782, 1785
Norfolk, 1785
Northumberland, 1782, 1784
Orange, 1782, 1785
Pittsylvania, 1782, 1785
Powhatan, 1783
Prince Edward, 1783, 1785
Princess Anne, 1783, 1785
City of Richmond, 1782
Richmond, 1783

Rockingham, 1784
Shenandoah, 1783, 1785
Stafford, 1785
Surry, 1782, 1784
Sussex, 1782
Warwick, 1782, 1784
City of Williamsburg, 1782

Supplementing the Census Bureau's reconstructed 1790 census is a work which was developed from the personal property tax lists of residents of all the missing counties: Augusta B. Fothergill and John M. Naugle, *Virginia Tax Payers 1782-87, Other Than Those Published by the United States Census Bureau* (1940, repr. Baltimore, 1971). However, the most comprehensive substitute for the missing 1790 census - also compiled from tax lists - is Netti Schreiner-Yantis, *The 1787 Census of Virginia,* 3 vols. (Springfield, VA, 1987).

All of the original records of these early Virginia censuses can be found at:

> Virginia State Library and Archives
> 11th Street at Capitol Square
> Richmond, Virginia 23219-3491

WASHINGTON

The territorial and state censuses are available at:

Washington State Archives
P.O. Box 9000
12th and Washington Streets
Olympia, Washington 98504-0418

Territorial censuses for Washington were taken at various times between 1857 and 1892. These censuses were taken by the officials of each county, who decided how to record the information and how often to take the census. The information contained in these censuses may vary slightly, but generally includes surname, given name or initials, age, sex, race, occupation, marital status, place of birth, and citizenship. Enumerations were made of whites, blacks, mulattoes, Kanakas, Indian half-breeds, and Chinese, though not of full blood Native Americans. Often the Chinese were lumped into the category "so many Chinese."

The federal government took censuses in Washington Territory in 1850, 1860, 1870, and 1880. These were in the same format as the federal censuses of these years. Ronald Vern Jackson (AIS) has published indexes for all four of these censuses.

Microfilms of the territorial and state censuses are available on interlibrary loan from the Washington State Library (Capitol Campus, State Library Building, Washington/Northwest Room, Olympia, Washington 98504) or by purchase from the Washington State Archives. Individual rolls are $15.00 and the complete 20-roll set is $300.00. The Washington State Archives will do a quick search (one individual, one county, one year) for no fee except a $.25 per page copying charge.

The following is a list of counties and the years for which there are territorial and state censuses available at the Washington State Archives. Those also available at the FHL have been noted:

Adams: 1885, 1887, 1889 (FHL)
Asotin: 1885, 1887, 1889 (FHL)
Chehalis: 1858, 1860, 1871, 1885
Clallam: 1857, 1860, 1871, 1883, 1885, 1887, 1889 (at FHL, but not on Archives list)
Clark: 1857, 1860, 1871, 1883, 1885, 1887

Columbia: 1883, 1885, 1887, 1889 (FHL)
Cowlitz: 1871, 1883, 1885, 1887 (all at FHL)
Douglas: 1885, 1887 (at FHL, but not on Archives list), 1892
Franklin: 1885, 1887 (both at FHL)
Garfield: 1883, 1885, 1887, 1889, 1892, 1898
Island: 1857, 1860, 1871, 1883, 1885, 1887, 1889 (at FHL, but not on Archives list)
Jefferson: 1860, 1871, 1874, 1877, 1878, 1879, 1880, 1881, 1883, 1885, 1887, 1889 (FHL), 1891
King: 1856, 1871, 1879 (FHL), 1880, 1881, 1883, 1885, 1887, 1889, 1892
Kitsap: 1857, 1860, 1871, 1883, 1885, 1887, 1889
Kittitas: 1885, 1887, 1889 (all at FHL)
Klickitat: 1871, 1883, 1885, 1887, 1889, 1892 (all at FHL)
Lewis: 1857, 1860, 1871, 1883, 1885, 1887
Lincoln: 1885, 1887, 1889 (FHL)
Mason: 1857, 1871, 1879, 1883, 1885, 1887, 1889 (FHL), 1892
Pacific: 1883, 1885, 1887 (FHL)
Pierce: 1857, 1871, 1878, 1879, 1883, 1885, 1887, 1889 (FHL), 1892
San Juan: 1885, 1887, 1889 (FHL)
Skagit: 1885, 1887 (both at FHL)
Skamania: 1860, 1871, 1885 (FHL), 1887 (FHL)
Snohomish: 1883, 1885, 1887, 1889 (FHL)
Spokane: 1885, 1887
Stevens: 1871, 1878, 1885, 1887, 1892
Thurston: 1871, 1873, 1875, 1877, 1878, 1879, 1880, 1881, 1883, 1885, 1887, 1889 (FHL), 1892
Wahkiakum: 1857, 1885, 1887
Walla Walla: 1885, 1887 (FHL), 1892 (FHL)
Whatcom: 1860 (FHL), 1871 (FHL), 1885 (FHL), 1887 (FHL), 1889
Whitman: 1883, 1885, 1887, 1889
Yakima: 1871, 1883, 1885, 1887 (all at FHL)

Some of these censuses have been published by Dolores Dunn Ackerman, Stack Enterprises, 3235 Alderwood, Bellingham, WA 98225.

Adams County, 1889 (1986)
Asotin County, 1889 (1986)
Chehalis (now called Grays Harbor), 1885 (1985)
Columbia, 1889 (1986)
Douglas, 1887 (1986)
Franklin, 1885 and 1887 (1986)
Island, 1889 (1986)
Island, 1887 and 1892 (to be published in 1992 or 1993)

Jefferson, 1889 (1989)
Kitsap, 1889 (1991)
Lewis, 1889 (1990)
Lincoln, 1889 (1987)
Mason, 1889 (1986)
Pacific, 1887 (1989)
San Juan, 1889 (1986)
Skagit, 1889 (1989)
Snohomish, 1889 (1986)
Wahkiakum, 1887 (1991)
Walla Walla, 1887 (1986)

Other published counties are:

Jeanne Polumsky Coe, *Auditor's Census - 1885-1887-1889 - Index to Asotin County, Washington* (1986); write to author at West 2225 Gardner, Spokane, WA 99201.

Clallam, 1857 (date unknown) and *Census of the Inhabitants in the County of Clallum, Territory of Washington, 1889* (1989), Clallam County Genealogical Society, ^c/o Clallam County Museum, 223 East Fourth Street, Port Angeles, WA 98362.

Ruby Simonson McNeill, *Columbia County, Washington Territorial Census, 1889* (1980); write to author at P.O. Box 779, Napavine, WA 98565.

Cowlitz County, Washington Territory, Auditor's Census with Surname Index, 1871, 1883, 1885, 1887 (1985), Lower Columbia Genealogical Society, P.O. Box 472, Longview, WA 98632.

"Garfield County 1887, 1889, 1898, 1902," *Washington State Genealogical and Historical Review*, vol. 3 (1986).

"Jefferson County, 1881," *Jefferson County Genealogical Society Bulletin*, vols. 4 and 5.

Territorial Census, Jefferson County, Territory of Washington, 1889 (1989), Jefferson County Genealogical Society, 210 Madison, Port Townsend, WA 98368.

Marjorie C. Rhodes, *1871 Territorial Census for King County, Washington (Enumerated July 25, 1871)* (1986) and *1879 Territorial Census for King County, Washington* (1988); write to author at 8521 17th Avenue N.E., Seattle, WA 98115.

Ballard Census of 1890 [King County] (1989) and *West Seattle Census of 1907 [King County]* (1989), Seattle Genealogical Society, P.O. Box 1708, Seattle, WA 98111.

Kittitas County 1885-1887-1889, Washington Territorial Censuses (1982), Yakima Valley Genealogical Society, P.O. Box 455, Yakima, WA 98907.

Kitsap, 1889 Territorial Census (date unknown), Kitsap County Historical Museum, 3343 N.W. Byron, Silverdale, WA 98383.

Jack M. Lines, *Klickitat County Territorial Census, 1871, 1882, 1885, 1887, 1889* (1983), Yakima Valley Genealogical Society, P.O. Box 455, Yakima, WA 98907.

Linda Patton and Darlene Stone, *Lewis County 1871 Census* (1979); write to Linda Patton, 435 Avery Road East, Chehalis, WA 98532; they plan to publish the 1883 Lewis County census in 1992.

Leland J. Athow, "Pierce 1854," *The Researcher, Tacoma/Pierce County Genealogical Society Bulletin*, vol. 25; write to TCGS, P.O. Box 1952, Tacoma, WA 98402.

1889 Auditor's Census of Pierce County, Washington (1987), Tacoma/Pierce County Genealogical Society, P.O. Box 1952, Tacoma, WA 98402.

"San Juan, 1887" and "San Juan, 1889," *Whatcom Genealogical Society Bulletin*, vols. 6 and 16; write to WGS, P.O. Box 1493, Bellingham, WA 98227.

1885 Census of Skagit County, Washington Territory (1986), Whatcom Genealogical Society, P.O. Box 1493, Bellingham, WA 98227.

Daphne Ramsay, *Skamania County, Washington, Census Records 1867, 1870, 1880, 1885, 1887* (1987), Clark County Genealogical Society, P.O. Box 2728, Vancouver, WA 98668.

"Snohomish County, 1861," *Washington State Genealogical and Historical Review*, vol. 4 (1983).

"Snohomish City Census, 1862," *The Sounder*, vol. 1; write to Sno-Isle Genealogical Society, P.O. Box 63, Edmonds, WA 98020.

Rai Cammack, *Washington Territorial Census Spokane County, 1887* (1990); write to author at Route 2, Box 50A, Potlatch, ID 83855.

1889 Census Thurston County, Washington Territory (1987), Olympia Genealogical Society, Olympia Timberland Library, Eighth and Franklin, Olympia, WA 98501.

Whatcom 1885, 1887, 1889 (date unknown), Whatcom Genealogical Society, P.O. Box 1493, Bellingham, WA 98227.

Whitman County 1883, 1885, 1887, 1889; to be published in 1992 by the Whitman County Genealogical Society, P.O. Box 393, Pullman, WA 99163.

Jack M. Lines, *Yakima County Territorial Censuses 1871-1883-1885-1887, Including Benton County, Founded in 1905; Including 1871-1883 Kittitas and Chelan Counties (Kittitas Founded in 1883, Chelan in 1889)* (1986), Yakima Valley Genealogical Society, P.O. Box 455, Yakima, WA 98907

Many thanks to Sarah Thorson Little for her help with this section.

WISCONSIN

The state censuses are available at:

The State Historical Society of Wisconsin
816 State Street
Madison, Wisconsin 53706-1488

Researchers may be interested in obtaining *Genealogical Research, An Introduction to the Resources of the State Historical Society of Wisconsin*, edited by James P. Danky (Madison, 1986) for further information on Wisconsin records.

Wisconsin took the following state censuses:

1836: Names the head of household, the number of males under 21, number of males over 21, number of females under 21, and number of females over 21. This census included the area which was later set off as Iowa Territory in 1838. The portion covering what became Wisconsin was published as "The Territorial Census for 1836" in *Wisconsin Historical Collections*, 13:247-270. An index has been published by Ronald Vern Jackson, *Wisconsin 1836 Census Index* (AIS, 1976).

1838: Names the master, mistress, steward, overseer, or other principal person; name of head of family; number of white males; number of white females; number of free males of color; number of free females of color. Only portions of this census still exist. The following are the counties for which there are complete schedules: Brown, Calumet (part of Brown), Crawford, Dodge, Fond du Lac (part of Brown), Green, Jefferson, Manitowoc (part of Brown), Marquette (part of Brown), Milwaukee, Portage (part of Brown), Sheboygan (part of Brown), Washington. An index has been published by Ronald Vern Jackson, *Wisconsin 1838 Census Index* (AIS, 1984).

1842: Contains the same information as 1838. An index has been published by Ronald Vern Jackson, *Wisconsin 1842 Census Index* (AIS, 1984).

1846: Names the head of family, number of white males, number of white females, number of colored males, and number of colored females. Schedules are lacking for Crawford County, Fond du Lac County, Grand Rapids in Portage County, and Sheboygan County. No schedules from the counties of Chippewa, LaPointe, and Richland.

1847: Contains the same information as 1846. Schedules lacking for the counties of Rock, Sheboygan, Washington, and Waukesha. No schedules from Chippewa County.

1855: Names the head of family, number of white males, number of white females, number of colored males, number of colored females, number of deaf and dumb, blind or insane, number of individuals in each household of foreign birth. Kewaunee County was not enumerated. The Northwoods Genealogy Society, P.O. Box 1132, Rhinelander, Wisconsin 54501, has prepared an index to this census. They will search for $2.00 per surname. An index has been published by Ronald Vern Jackson, *Wisconsin 1855 Census Index* (AIS, 1984).

1865: The state copies of the schedules for the 1865 census were destroyed. County copies are available for the following counties: Dunn, Green, Jackson, Kewaunee, Ozaukee, Sheboygan.

1875: Names the head of family, number of white males, number of females, number of colored males, number of colored females, number of deaf and dumb, blind or insane.

1885: Names the head of family, number of white males, number of white females, number of colored males, number of colored females, number born in each of the following countries: United States, Great Britain, Ireland, France, British America, Scandinavia, Holland, all other countries. This census also includes a special enumeration of "Soldiers and Sailors of the Late War." For each veteran it includes his name, rank, company and regiment, state from which he served, and his post office address.

1895: Contains the same information as 1885, and also includes the veterans' schedule.

1905: Names each individual, relationship to the head of household, color or race, sex, age at last birthday, marital status, place of birth (state or country), place of birth of parents (state or country), occupation for all age 14 or over, number of months employed, whether home or farm is owned (mortgaged or clear) or rented. This census also includes a special enumeration of "Soldiers and Sailors of the Late War."

Many thanks to James L. Hansen for his help with this section.

WYOMING

Wyoming began taking state censuses in 1905, but these are purely statistical. The headings on these records vary from page to page and include statistics on agriculture (crops), minerals, and population by towns. They are organized by county. No names are included. Many of these will still be found in the individual county seats while others will be found at:

> Wyoming State Archives and Historical Department
> Barrett Building
> Cheyenne, Wyoming 82002

Also at the State Archives are censuses for the city of Cheyenne taken in 1875 and 1878 which include name, age, sex, birthplace, occupation, and nationality of resident.

Many thanks to Virginia Wakefield for her help with this section.